HOW TO AVOID CROWDS

Travel smart and enjoy your vacation without overtourism

(Plus a chapter on traveling during and after the coronavirus pandemic)

TABLE OF CONTENTS

INTRODUCTION

Over the last few decades, tourism has changed. It has become too busy and vacations are not as enjoyable as they used to be. When we travel, we're surrounded by tens of thousands of fellow travelers. Beaches, cities, and landmarks have become so crowded that there is seemingly no more room for a stress-free and crowd-free vacation. When the situation gets so bad that we're not able to enjoy it anymore, we call it "overtourism". Unfortunately, overtourism is now everywhere.

But there is also good news. Even the most busy, most beloved destinations can be visited without the masses if you know when to go. Tourism comes in waves, and those waves are highly predictable. Our job is to predict these waves.

In 2019, my wife and myself launched a website that can tell you how busy the world's most popular tourist destinations will be on any given day. Within months, our initiative—Avoid-Crowds.com—had caught the attention of some of the world's biggest publications including *The Washington Post, Los Angeles Times,* CNN and dozens of other media outlets around the world. In this book, we're sharing our secrets with you. By combining hard data with common knowledge and our own experiences, we'll explain how tourism works and when to expect the biggest crowds and we'll share how, even on the busiest days, you can still avoid them. With this book, you can become a smarter tourist, so that you can even enjoy traveling in the age of overtourism.

Travel today comes with other problems that just didn't exist 20 years, five years, or even a year ago, before COVID-19 began disrupting everything. We are still in the midst of the coronavirus pandemic as we write this book, but as borders opened up again within Europe, we started traveling again. We want to share our experience of how the new normal looked and felt as we stayed at eight hotels in five different countries. As well as giving you tips and tricks on how to even enjoy the most crowded days, we'll also help you to try to make sense of travel in the post-pandemic world.

The original idea came to us while we were walking down the gangway of the biggest cruise ship in the world, into a city that wasn't able to handle it. As we walked among 6,000 other cruise passengers into Barcelona, our eyes were opened to the problem of overtourism. And we were part of it. It was a moment that inspired a website that tackles overtourism head on.

Although we'd been confronted with mass tourism before, our Barcelona cruise experience was the first time overtourism hit us right in the face. As we walked into the Port of Barcelona, Europe's most frequently visited cruise port, tens of thousands of tourists from numerous other ships were doing the exact same thing. Almost like a military invasion, our ships arrived at exactly the same time, opening their doors to thousands of passengers who rushed off to occupy parts of the city. But, as we experienced throughout the day, it was so much worse than just busy. These tourists were not evenly spread across the city; most of them had left their different ships with exactly the same itinerary in their pockets.

Cruise passengers can be easily recognized. Passengers on an organized schedule will wear a numbered sticker referring to their group tour number. Apparently, sticker-wearing cruise passengers are only interested in the major attractions, which makes sense because they only have one day. In fact, they only have a small part of the day, as they have to be back on the ship before 4 p.m. That means that thousands of tourists want to see the same sights and they will have the same day program. In Barcelona, that program is limited to the famous Sagrada Família, Gaudí's Park Güell, the Gothic Quarter, and a walk on Las Ramblas. On our busy cruise day, the tourists hit the city like an inferno. Traffic around the harbor came to a complete standstill, long lines formed at the tourist attractions, and the narrow streets of the old Gothic Quarter were blocked by tour groups.

Barcelona suffered heavily from mass tourism that day, but it was not only Barcelona that was suffering. On that same day, cities and towns in other parts of the Mediterranean were overcrowded as well. Venice, Rome, Dubrovnik, and other destinations all received more cruise passengers than they are really able to handle. Cities across the European continent and beyond were suffering as a result of their own success. Too many tourists wanted to experience the beauty for which they are famous.

On that September day in 2016, we were passengers on the biggest cruise ship in the world: *Harmony of the Seas*. The cruise ship brought us from Civitavecchia near Rome to Naples, Mallorca, Barcelona, Marseille and La Spezia. A day after La Spezia, which is often promoted as the port of the wildly popular Cinque Terre, we arrived back at our starting point. Later we found out that—with some changing destinations—this is one of the most heavily used cruise routes in the world. Known as the Western Mediterranean route, it takes passengers to Europe's most visited cruise destinations. A similar thing happens about 5,000 miles to the west, where a Caribbean cruise route takes passengers to the two of the three busiest cruise destinations in the world: Cozumel in Mexico and Nassau in the Bahamas. If that cruise starts and ends in Miami, passengers complete the full top three.

As we were on Europe's busiest cruise route, it can be no surprise that our ship was never alone. Everywhere our cruise ship docked, with over 6,000 cruise passengers and 2,300 crew members, it was accompanied by multiple other large cruise ships. On some of these days, over 30,000 cruise passengers set foot in the local towns that were on our itinerary. To put that in perspective, Venice's historical center only has around 50,000 people actually living in it.

But back to the 30,000 cruise passengers we were part of; it's important to consider that these 30,000 cruise passengers come on top of all the tourists that arrive at the same destination by airplane, car, bus, and train. The overall tourist footprint is usually much bigger than "just" those cruise ships. Some destinations were already overrun by tourists before the cruise ship industry really got going. The addition of our fellow passengers and ourselves to these overcrowded places did not contribute to the experience. Our one-day excursion to Palma de Mallorca was a particular disappointment.

The experience opened our eyes. For the first time, we'd been fully exposed to mass tourism. After we returned from our vacation, I started to research. I wanted to understand what influences mass tourism. Questions about tourism started to play a big role in our lives. Why do people visit some places more than others? Where are all these tourists coming from?

Does tourism change its destination? When are these tourists on vacation? The most important question for me and my wife was: how can we still visit these beloved destinations but without the crowds? In other words, how can we predict crowds so we can avoid them?

Our website, Avoid-Crowds.com, was born.

As we started to look into the answers, we came to the unfortunate discovery that information about tourism is scattered and often wrong, but tourism itself turned out to be incredibly predictable. Cruise ship companies make the schedules for their cruises years in advance. Families can only go on vacation when their kids are not in school so tracking school vacations and public holidays is key. There are obvious travel patterns as some regions in Europe attract more Germans, while others attract more British tourists. We also discovered that domestic travel is the biggest driver of tourism in most of Europe. Putting all that information together allows us to predict peaks.

But knowing when it is busy is not enough. Tourism has changed rapidly over the last ten years. It's far busier than ever before. Without smart planning, your trip to destinations that have become overcrowded will feel fake and you'll have less fun. You need to think more about your vacation in advance than you ever did before. If you do, you can still visit crowded destinations like Barcelona, Rome, or Venice and enjoy the experience from beginning to end. Even the most typical tourist experiences, like viewing the Mona Lisa, walking Las Ramblas, or touring the Colosseum, can be yours without standing in line for hours.

This book, was inspired by an article titled "We're in the age of the overtourist. You can avoid being one of them" that was published in *The Washington Post* in June 2019. It was written by travel journalist Hannah Sampson. At the time, we had just released our website, Avoid-Crowds.com, and were predicting tourism flows for about 30 European cities. Sampson interviewed my wife who vividly explained our vision and the reason we'd launched our website. The article created a chain reaction. Traffic to our website took off, which resulted in additional news coverage from around the world. The article was followed by coverage in newspapers around the world, CNN.com linked viewers to our site, and websites in countries like Hungary and New Zealand wrote about us in articles about overtourism. All of that would have taken much longer and been much more difficult without that phone call with Hannah Sampson. I continue to wonder whether we would have given up without Hannah, who we met through Twitter.

From September 2019 onward, we were preparing for the breakthrough year of Avoid-Crowds.com. Overtourism was a problem that was getting worse and worse and all seemed set for 2020 to become the busiest year on record. But, as we all know now, 2020 turned out to be a little different. As I write this book, the streets of Rome and Barcelona are quiet. In Paris, the famous Louvre Museum has closed its doors and the elevators at the Eiffel Tower are standing still. The canals of Venice, notorious for their pollution, are so clean that those living in the city can see fish swimming in them. Tourists, however, cannot see the fish swimming through the canals. Tourists are staying at home. Not because of overtourism, but because of COVID-19.

Where local governments and action groups have failed to stop the tourists from coming, the coronavirus has succeeded in putting an abrupt halt to travel across the globe. Airline tickets are no longer being sold and hotel beds remain empty. The number of visitors to our website, in what was set to be its breakthrough year, logically plummeted.

But the virus is also an opportunity to rethink how we want to travel and how we go on vacation, and this book is our small contribution to that. We'll walk you through what makes cities and other tourist destinations busy, and what the best months, weeks and days are to visit beloved spots around the world. We'll also explain how you can manage to have a great experience even on the busiest days. There are tips and tricks driven by data and common sense. If you're willing to adapt to modern-day travel, you will have an amazing experience as soon as the COVID-19 travel restrictions are lifted, and it's once again safe to do what we love: exploring and experiencing the beauty our world has to offer.

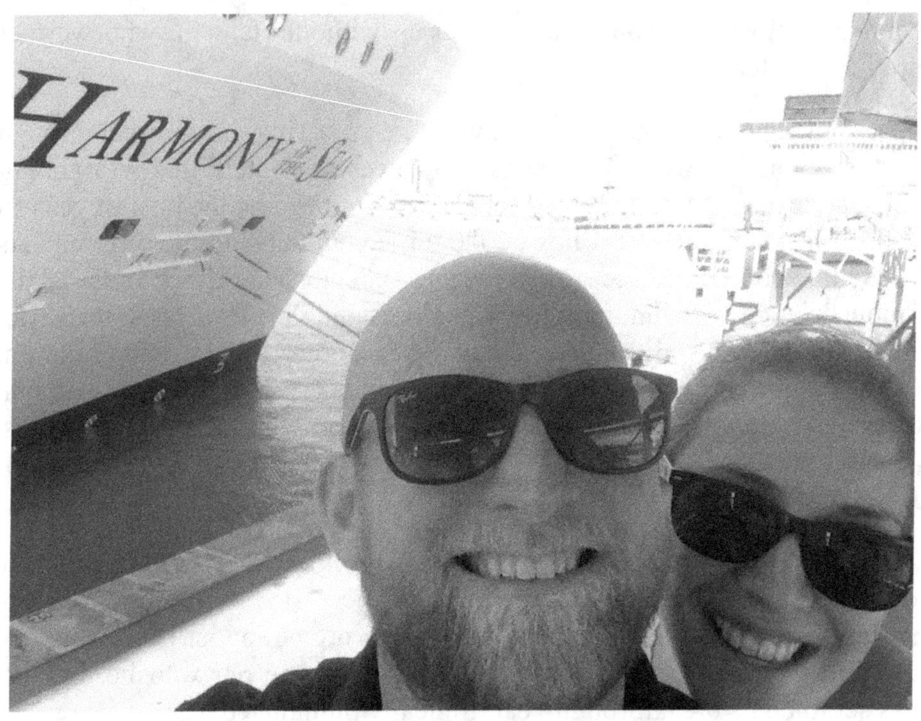

Mandy and myself taking a selfie with the cruise ship that inspired the website and book.

Book structure

This book is written as a non-fiction travel self-help book. Each chapter stands by itself and there is no beginning and end to this book. Throughout the book it is my intention to explain to you why some days, weeks or months are busier than others. You can go back and forth in the book or read it from the beginning. There is no single story that I tell throughout the book. I use personal experiences to make data, which I fear can be a bit boring, more accessible.

We start the book by explaining that the best time to travel really depends on your preferences. After that we explain the different travel seasons. That means we explore peak season, the two shoulder seasons and the low season. After you know the basics about when crowds come to our most beloved travel destinations, we start explaining in more detail what causes crowds.

The dark side of tourism is next: overtourism. In this chapter, I will go through all the negative side-effects of tourism but will also explain how you can make a positive impact or at least minimize the negative impact that you have when traveling.

Avoiding crowds while traveling covers the days when it is already busy. In this chapter I explain how you can still enjoy a crowd free holiday during the busiest days of the year. I also explain a bit on hotel prices and how you can get more favourable rates. If you make it even further in the book, we start talking about how you can recognize and avoid tourist traps, how to do your research and what tickets you can buy.

Since this book is written in 2020, we cannot talk about tourism without touching upon COVID-19. Luckily, my wife and I travelled throughout Europe in the summer of the pandemic between the first and second wave. Combined with some serious research we explain what you can expect when we travel during and after the pandemic. We cover airplanes, hotels and tourist attractions. At the end of the book you can find our global travel calendar. This is a month by month overview that shows you the best places to go around the world based on both weather and crowd predictions.

Throughout the book you learn about modern day traveling and dodging the world's biggest crowds. Although this book explains how to avoid crowds around the world, most of our examples are from Europe. Nevertheless, all our European examples are applicable elsewhere in the world. The same goes the other way around. We for example explain how tickets at One World Observatory work with timed entry. The same works elsewhere.

Thank you for picking up or downloading our book. I hope it will help you travel smarter and also hope my anecdotes brings a smile to your face.

WHEN IS THE BEST TIME TO TRAVEL?

To avoid crowds, you need to understand when tourists travel. This was the first step that we had to take if we wanted to build a website that predicts tourist crowds in the same way a weather forecast could predict the rain. Armed with that data, we could analyze the best time to travel to tourist destinations around the world.

To get there, we needed to gather data that tells us when mass tourism hits certain destinations. As the idea was born on a cruise vacation, cruise ship traffic felt like the natural place to start. We also decided to add information about local events. As a football (soccer) fan, I traveled quite a lot, following AFC Ajax from Amsterdam as they played all across the continent. As soon as the fans showed up in town, it became extremely busy. And many of Europe's major tourist destinations are homes to great football clubs. And so, based on our own experiences, we came up with two initial datasets: cruise arrivals and events.

The first dataset turned out to be easy to get. Cruise schedules are published online years before the ship sails, as cruise companies need to sell staterooms well in advance. Local event data is a little trickier to get. It requires constant and proactive searching and a good understanding of cities. There are some usual suspects: marathons, conferences, sports events and gay pride parades. Before we were able to automate some of this research, that meant googling everything, and without an ad blocker or incognito browser, we started to get targeted with all kinds of ads that were not made for us. I am not a runner but my search behavior makes Google and Amazon think differently. Nowadays, I am frequently targeted with ads for running shoes, running apps or three-day trips to run the New York City Marathon. The targeted ads hit a definite low when I was bombarded with ads for the away shirt of London-based football club Tottenham Hotspur—the team that kicked my beloved AFC Ajax out of the Champions League with a shocking comeback. Even now I still can't bear to watch the highlights. I remember that green jersey vividly, and don't want to see it ever again!

Armed with event and cruise data, we could now explain peaks in tourist arrivals in any given city. But we still couldn't explain why August is extremely busy in Barcelona and not so busy in South Florida. We needed other data to explain seasonal trends. Luckily for us, there are multiple organizations around the world that publish data about tourism for free. One of the most important sources of information we found was Eurostat, the statistics bureau of the European Union. Data from Eurostat is accessible for free and can be reused. It turned out to be a gold mine. With Eurostat's data, and other freely available data, we were able to understand travel patterns across Europe and the world. For each European destination, we could now say it would be busy for some months—for example, in the summer—and quiet in, for example, November. We also discovered that November and January are two of the quietest travel months in the world.

With all that data, we would finally be able to answer the question "when is the best time to travel?" Or so we thought…

Defining the best time to travel is both simple and difficult. It's a question that is so incredibly personal, that it requires lots of counter questions before we can answer it. The only right answer to that question is "it depends". It depends because some people actually like massive crowds. I used to be one of those people too.

Growing up in the Netherlands, my favorite vacation as a young adult was not a cultural city trip to Barcelona, or a beach vacation at an exotic destination. When I was a teenager, my favorite vacation was a party week in the famous coastal towns of the Costa Brava and Costa Daurada areas of Spain. These areas, located north and south of Barcelona, are famous party locations attracting massive crowds of youngsters from all over Europe. A good vacation for me was a week of partying on the beach in Lloret de Mar, bungee jumping, and drinking in Spanish clubs with fellow teenagers from around Europe. These trips were our European version of spring break, even if they happened in summer.

In 2003 when I was 18, I traveled to Lloret de Mar with a group of friends. Back then, bus companies were still in competition with airlines and those long bus rides were a much cheaper way to travel. Since we preferred to spend our money on cheap beer and shots, we chose the cheapest means of transportation over the most comfortable one. That's how we found ourselves on a 24-hour bus journey that started in Leiden, a university town 40 kilometers (25 miles) south of Amsterdam. The journey would start with several buses gathering tourists from all over the Netherlands and bringing them to a central hub in the country. At that hub, normally in the southern part of the country, you would wait for hours until each bus had arrived from different parts of the country. After all the buses had arrived, the real journey would start. Together with hundreds of other vacationers, you would search for your designated buses and start the journey to Spain. On the way, the bus would drive through Belgium, take a detour to Luxembourg to stop for cheap gas, and then continue through France to the Spanish border, which we would cross at around 5 a.m. About two hours later, the buses would arrive in Lloret de Mar.

From the windows of our buses, we would witness the last clubs and bars closing down after a long night and would see young adults, often teenagers like us, staggering through streets covered in dirt and the occasional pool of vomit in a drunken attempt to find their hotels and apartments. Meanwhile, Spanish authorities were starting to clean up the warzone by hosing down the streets with water, removing all proof of a night many of our peers would not be able to remember anyway. We loved it. That is exactly why we had come. We wanted to be the heroes of the night that would welcome the buses of teenagers that would replace us in a week's time.

The bus ride itself was fun; the catering on the bus included cold beers and you would have fun with your friends on the journey. The downside of all that fun was that you arrived in your destination already deprived of sleep. Just like the drunks finding their way to the hotels, we were ready to hit our beds ourselves. But those beds would have to wait. Tourists had until noon to check out, which meant that we were only allowed to check in at 3 or 4 p.m. And every hotel bed was filled because it was peak season—another reason why we were there, as a party vacation without other party people was not worthwhile. While the Costa Brava is beautiful, we wouldn't have chosen Lloret de Mar if we weren't there to party.

As I've grown older, I can look back at great memories from the Lloret de Mar years but I don't want to go back. Spring break style vacations are well behind me. I've outgrown foam parties and death-defying bungee jumps, and I certainly do not like looking at vomit. Like many others, my preferences have changed as I got older.

Changes in our lives usually lead to new, different expectations. It's exactly the same for vacations. We start to prefer different types of vacations as we grow older and our financial possibilities change. As a teenager, this type of vacation is all we saved money for. While we did a cultural day trip to Barcelona, most of our days were focused on partying. Nowadays, I still occasionally visit the area, but the vacations are not the same. I want to visit all the cultural highlights of the city instead; Park Güell, the Sagrada Família, and the Gothic Quarter are now our favorites. If we travel outside of Barcelona, it's to visit the Salvador Dalí House in Portlligat which, funnily enough, is closer to Lloret de Mar than Barcelona.

Not only did my preference in tourist attractions or "things to do" on vacation change, but also my perception of mass tourism and large crowds. As a teenager, I needed those events and tourist crowds to fill all the clubs and bars and to create the atmosphere for a good party. As an adult, I no longer like massive crowds, which have only gotten bigger since 2003. Now, I want to visit the Louvre Museum when I'm in Paris or find a quiet corner of Venice when we're in the city. I want to actively avoid any large crowds and absolutely hate wasting any time waiting in line on vacation. I still enjoy a good conversation with fellow tourists or local residents, and I don't want to travel completely alone. I don't want to party until 5 a.m., but do like to have conversations with fellow tourists.

The point of this story is that preferences change over time and that people change. Some people enjoy museums, while others enjoy going to foam parties. For some people, like me, those preferences might change from year to year depending on who they're traveling with. All of that means that the best time to travel is not the same for everybody. Party animals will need big crowds and for them peak season is perfect. For those seeking a cultural escape, long lines and huge crowds are the enemy. Low season is better for those tourists. Others, like families with children, often have no choice but to travel in peak season as they can only travel during breaks from school.

SEASONS

Peak season

For most travelers, the idea of large crowds of tourists is unattractive. In the wake of the COVID-19 crisis, the idea of long lines—where people cannot keep their distance and the chance of infections is high—is not just unappealing, it has become dangerous. Even so, during peak season in 2020 there were still plenty of reports of overcrowded beaches, full bars and infections rising again as a result. While in "normal" times, understanding peak season and when to avoid crowds is a luxury, during a pandemic it is an absolute necessity.

Peak season, or high season, is the period of time in which tourist destinations are busiest. That doesn't mean it is de facto the worst time to travel. There are pros to counter the cons of overcrowding and there are often compromises to be made. You'll probably have to choose between small crowds or good weather. If you want small crowds in Italy or Greece, then you should go in winter. If you want to have beautiful weather during your vacation and still visit those popular destinations, you're going to have to cope with crowds. If you want both sunny weather and small crowds, you probably need to adjust your expectations or visit places that are less frequently visited by tourists. The same holds true for winter sports. Winter sports resorts will be busy when there is snow, but will be quieter when the sports cannot take place. We think this trade-off is crystal clear, and we want to manage expectations. If you don't like big crowds, do not travel in peak season. If you want good weather guaranteed or if you like to travel when most others are traveling, travel during peak season might be right for you.

In this chapter we'll explain more about what peak season is and when it is.

When is peak season?

To understand what peak season is, we need to explore why people travel. There are different reasons to travel and not all contribute to peak season. Firstly, and most importantly of all, is having the ability to travel. Travel is a luxury that most people want but many cannot afford to the extent they might wish. More than money, travel is influenced by the ability to take days off of work. While the average number of paid vacation days for an employee in the United States is only 15 days, European workers have a minimum of 20 paid vacation days. In most countries, employees enjoy considerably more than that.

Even the luckiest employees, however, often cannot freely use these days as they would like. They can't simply wake up one morning and pack their bags to go on a vacation. For one, their children's schools do not allow them to do so. Taking your children out of school during term time is a crime in some European countries. As a result, families often have little or no ability to travel outside school vacation periods.

And it's not just children that limit when people can travel. Sometimes entire industries, like construction workers in the Netherlands or Belgium, all get their vacation at the same time. One widespread example of this seasonal industry stop is parliaments and governments around the world, who will shut their doors for weeks at a time. The United States Congress recesses for the month of August. The European Parliament gets a similar traditional summer break from the third week of July to the third week of August. The impact of having a few hundred politicians going on vacation is not that big by itself, but the number of workers that surround the institutions of government is huge. Think about all those lobbyists, political journalists, and support staff (including caterers as well as office workers) with nothing to do for well over a month.

When we started comparing school vacations around the world with hotel occupancy rates, we found that the two closely correlated. In simple terms, when schools closed for a vacation, the number of occupied hotel beds went up. Weather patterns have a similar correlation; when the sun shines, more hotel beds are occupied. But sudden peaks in October, December or February couldn't be explained by the weather, and neither could the rise in reservations around Easter or Pentecost. While we were able to find multiple metrics that correlated to increasing numbers of hotel reservations, the only plausible causation for increasing tourist arrivals was school vacations. We'd discovered that the most important metric in predicting tourist crowds is to look at the schedules of schools. Mapping all school vacations was the next step in building Avoid-Crowds.com's data model. But, as always, it turned out to be much more complicated than that.

Not every school holiday had the same impact on each location. Some destinations were more popular among Germans, while others attracted more Americans, French, or Brits. The next part of making our data model was looking at the nationality of those arriving at each location. This required much more in-depth research. Fortunately, data from the European Union's statistics bureau Eurostat made this challenge a little easier.

It became clear that for most destinations we didn't even have to look beyond the country's borders. Interestingly, it's not international tourism that is the biggest contributor to how busy tourist destinations become. It's actually people traveling within a country—so-called domestic tourism— that contributes most to crowds of tourists. In every European country except Luxembourg, the majority of hotel rooms are occupied by domestic tourists. That means that for example Italians prefer to stay in Italy for a vacation. The same holds true for the United States: Americans don't necessarily leave their country when they leave their homes.

And that was the case even before the COVID-19 crisis. Travel restrictions no longer allow us to move freely across borders and until governments, medical professionals, and the travel industry have found solutions to the problems posed by the pandemic, domestic tourism will be more popular than ever before. Many governments, seeking ways to help the ailing travel industry, are now promoting domestic tourism or "staycations" as an alternative to traveling internationally. As a result, the coronavirus crisis is expected to increase the number of tourists opting for a vacation within their own national borders.

Of course, it's always been a different story at many destinations in the Mediterranean or Caribbean, where the local population is relatively small and the number of tourists sometimes outnumber those actually living there. Barcelona's statistics also tell a different story to the overall European numbers. Research by the local government[1], shows that only 12% of all hotel stays in Barcelona people living in Spain. Although that number doesn't take into account that many Spaniards visiting the city will do so on a day trip, it does show that it doesn't make sense only to look at domestic travel either. Luckily, the same research by the local government shows that the vast majority of international arrivals come from within the EU (51%). For Barcelona, local school vacations combined with European school vacations are perfect for predicting peak season.

At Avoid-Crowds.com, we take both domestic and international tourism arrivals into consideration when we predict how busy popular destinations like London will become. For the British capital, for example, we look at official data that is published by the Major of London that we feed into our models. The latest data on the website[2] shows some interesting trends when it comes to international tourism arrivals. First of all, tourism appears to peak in the third quarter, but is relatively spread out over the year. That makes London a year-round destination, though the cold winter months of January and February are definitely the quieter months. The biggest group of international travelers visiting London in 2018 came from the United States (14%) followed by France (10%), Germany (8%), Spain (7%), and Italy (5%). In fact, to predict 60% of international travel to London, we only need to look at travel factors in about 10 countries. Meanwhile, day-trippers and domestic tourism still account for the majority of tourists in London (41%)[3]. While London is the most popular destination for international tourists visiting the UK, its domestic tourism mainly consists of those living in urban areas visiting beaches and rural areas.

So what does this mean for the individual tourist? We discussed a lot of different datasets that are not easy to understand or easy to combine for tourists who are not interested in data. We have therefore combined all these different data points, such as cruise ship arrivals, school vacations and local events into a single score; the Avoid Crowds' crowd score. We give each day a score from 1 to 100. A crowd score of 1 means that a destination is not busy at all while 100 means that it is extremely crowded.

As shown in Figure 1, where we use our crowds score to visualize how busy a destination can get, August is clearly the busiest month of the year, closely followed by July. This is the result of school holidays in almost all countries. Pretty much all children on the European continent will be on vacation at the end of July and beginning of August. During these weeks, people enjoy family vacations, and Europe can get extremely busy. If you want to avoid being stuck in traffic surrounded by domestic tourists, it is best to watch out for local school vacations and national public holidays.

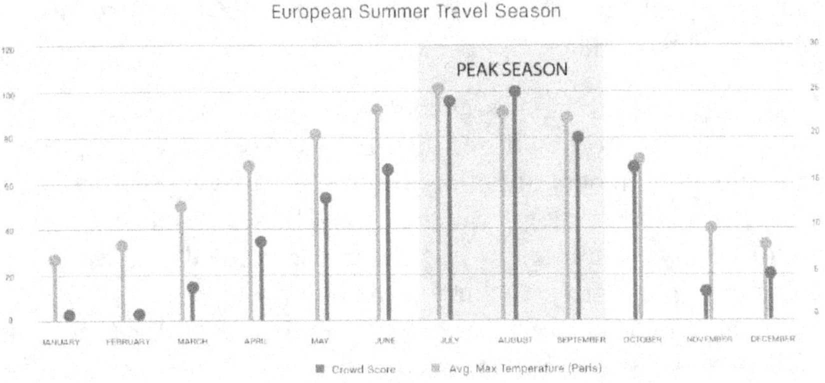

Figure 1: Peak Season. SOURCES: Avoid-Crowds.com's average crowd score per month. Weather source is Google and is displayed in degrees Celsius.

Business travel, on the other hand, takes place throughout the entire year, but slows down around summer and the holiday season. As a result, regular business travel doesn't need to be taken into consideration for determining the peak season. Conferences and business events, however, are a major contributor to how busy a destination can be. Web Summit, an annual tech conference in Portugal, attracts about 70,000 visitors to Lisbon. According to research by Deloitte[4], Lisbon has around 30,000 hotel rooms and short-term rentals like Airbnb combined. You can imagine the effect Web Summit has on the town. Add a major Champions League football (soccer) match to the mix and the city is packed. This is exactly what happened when AFC Ajax from Amsterdam played Lisbon's Benfica in November 2018.

Local governments usually try to promote travel outside peak season by organizing larger events outside the already busy peak season. This way, hotel beds that would otherwise remain empty would be filled with those attending events like marathons or large business conferences.

All this knowledge about domestic tourism, and the knowledge that most people travel during school vacations, allow us to determine when peak season is. Although there are different peak seasons around the world, the European and American summer season is what we would normally refer to as peak season. The summer travel season normally starts halfway through June and ends in early September. The first week of September means back to business for most of Europe while Labor Day (the first Monday in September) traditionally marks the end of the summer travel season in the United States.

In Europe, peak season is at its highest point from July to August. Airports around the world will see their busiest days halfway through peak season with high numbers of both returning and arriving tourists. In 2019, the busiest travel day of the year in the United States was the weekend after the Fourth of July[5]. In Europe, without specific national holidays that mark the beginning of summer, it's busy throughout July and August, but gets extremely busy at the end of July and beginning of August. Other statistics, such as how busy roads in Europe become during this time, back this up and show that August (in the Northern Hemisphere) is the busiest time for tourism. In other words, peak season peaks in August.

Destination	Peak Tourism Season
Europe	
Large European Cities (Rome, London, Paris)	Mid June to Early September
Alps	Christmas Holidays & February
	July and August
Mediterranean	Mid June to Early September
Nordics and Baltics	June to August
Eastern and Central Europe	June to August
Americas	
Larger Northern Cities (New York, Chicago, Boston)	June to September (effect somewhat mitigated as many families leave for the coast) and Christmas Holidays.
Coastal US (California, Hamptons)	July to August
Florida	December to April
Hawaii	December to April
Caribbean	December to April
Canada	July to September
Central America (Costa Rica)	December to April
South America (Brazil)	December to April
Others	
Australia	December to February
Bali	December to January July to August

*Figure 2: Peak Tourism Seasons around the world. *Tourists from Europe and the United States make up the majority of tourists across the globe. The summer months in the Northern Hemisphere (June to August) allow people to travel and, as a result, these months will see an increase in tourists at most destinations.*

Peak season for winter vacations

If you want to avoid crowds when you go skiing, it's obvious that July and August are not the right months to do so. While it's a lot less likely to be busy, it's also much less likely that there's any snow in the Alps during the year's hottest months. The winter sports season in the Northern Hemisphere starts in December and lasts until mid-April, but unlike the regular travel calendar, the winter sports season does not have just one peak.

Peak season on the slopes works slightly different, and the typical European winter sports season has two peaks. Thanks to snow cannons, ski resorts can more or less guarantee some form of skiing from the end of November onwards. Resort towns that are situated at higher altitudes may be open even earlier. But the big crowds will not arrive in the mountains until the December holidays. Ski resorts in both Europe and the US see their biggest crowds in the last weeks of the year, as many Europeans and Americans opt for a white Christmas in the mountains. It's busiest between Christmas and New Year's Eve.

On top of all those vacationers, the weather plays an important role in how busy ski resorts get. Those living near the mountains will look at the weather forecast before they decide to go skiing. In 2019, December 29 was the busiest day on record for ski areas in Salzburgerland, Austria and it was one of those perfect weather days. Austrian newspaper *Salzburger Nachrichten*[6] wrote that good weather and perfect snow conditions had attracted lots of day-trippers to the popular ski areas. Combined with a seasonal peak in vacationers, this last-minute influx resulted in some extremely crowded days on the Austrian slopes.

December is not only a busy time in the Alps and the Colorado mountains. It is a busy time almost everywhere. The Christmas holiday season is a unique time of the year when most people have time off work, which allows them to travel. Meanwhile, events such as the ball drop in Times Square and Christmas markets in Europe make cities a very attractive destination for travelers around the world. As a result, prices—including in winter sports areas—will rapidly rise over the Christmas break. Hotel beds and airfares will be even more expensive than during some of the summer's busiest weekends. But as soon as January arrives, those prices drop steeply as almost all of us return to our day jobs.

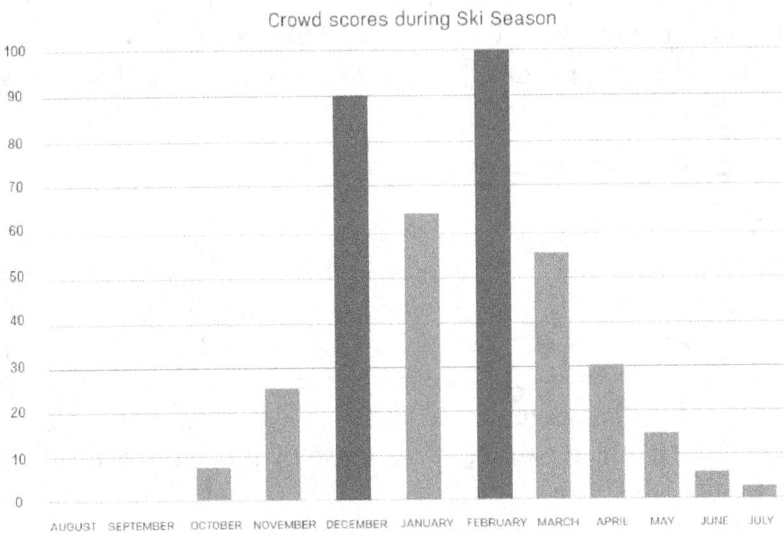

Figure 1: Ski season. SOURCE: Avoid-Crowds.com crowd score. 1 = not crowded, 100= extremely crowded.

This means that January is a relatively slow month for winter sports. It will never be completely empty, but the craziness of the overcrowded slopes during the Christmas break are behind us. During the month of January, it is mostly only busy on the weekends. In Europe, the tourists do come back for a second peak season, when the winter school holidays start in most of the northern and western European countries, including Switzerland and Austria. Halfway through February, the ski resorts get incredibly busy again as millions of tourists use this break from schools to go on winter sports vacations, causing the second peak.

When February is over, the ski season slowly burns out as warmer weather moves in. With the snow melting, the lower-situated ski areas stop their ski lifts first, followed by those higher up. Glaciers, situated at over 2,500 meters (8,200 feet) above sea level, will remain open well into the summer. If you want to ski with small crowds, March is the best month to travel. If you want to go for the Après Ski party experience, try the peak season weeks in December or February.

Insider tip: For Europe's ski areas, Saturday is a perfect day for skiing. Most tourists buy week packages, which means that they are

either leaving their accommodations or just arriving at the resort. Most tourists don't ski on these travel days, which makes the slopes a little quieter, even in peak season.

How does peak season impact you?

Peak season is busy. Hotels will be full, restaurants will have no problem filling their tables, and beaches will be crowded. In many European destinations, the streets and alleys will be so full that it's no longer possible to enjoy the streets at your own pace. One of the European destinations heavily impacted during peak season is Venice. The Italian city has become the poster child of overtourism. In 2010, I visited the city with my wife Mandy—then girlfriend—during peak season while on a road trip through Europe as students.

We borrowed my father's car and drove from Leiden in the Netherlands. In the old diesel-powered Peugeot 206, we set off for a European road trip that would take us through Germany, Austria, Italy, France, and Belgium. We left at the peak of peak season, July 24, and returned the first week of August. For most of the trip, we stayed at campsites as we had little money and preferred to spend that on experiences rather than somewhere we would only be sleeping. During this trip, we learned what peak season means and we got our first lessons in overtourism.

Our 3,200-kilometer (2,000-mile) trip started with a full day's drive to Munich. This drive—which was especially hard on Mandy, as I did not have a driving license back in 2010—took us through most of Europe with probably the worst possible timing. All Saturdays from mid-July to mid-August are extremely busy on European roads, but some are known as "the most terrible". The worst days are called "Samedi Noir" by the French, which unfortunately translates into the not so woke "Black Saturday". On Black Saturday, tourists will leave their homes in northwestern Europe and drive to the south and southeast. As a result, all of the major highways in France and the south of Germany are blocked. On Black Saturday, you need to be prepared to spend most of your time traveling to your dream vacation in one long traffic jam.

Little did we know that this was the day on which we'd planned our journey. Neither did we know, while we were waiting in a traffic jam in the most western part of Germany, that this vacation would be a crash course in the peak season and mass tourism.

Our first lesson was traffic. Traffic during peak season can be bad, especially on weekends. Our drive from the Netherlands to Munich should have taken us about eight or nine hours. In the end, it took us almost twice as long and we arrived in Munich after 15 and a half hours on the road. After surviving these long delays, we finally arrived in Munich where we had a hotel reservation at a hotel named King's Hotel Center, an affordable hotel located less than a 10-minute walk from the city center. We were soon to learn our second lesson.

Hungry from our long drive, we wanted to get something to eat quickly, but we arrived in the middle of a true cloudburst. As we left the hotel to go out for dinner, it had started raining heavily. All the tourists who'd enjoyed the weather earlier that day, escaped the deluge by ducking into Munich's restaurants and beer halls. There was literally not a single table—or even single seat—in any decent place. We tried four or five before giving up and returning to the hotel. That's how we learned our second lesson: not only is it busy on the roads, but also at your destination and you need to be ready to compete with your fellow tourists for tables. Reservations are key to having a proper experience. It wasn't all bad news. After returning to the hotel, we decided to grab something to eat at the hotel bar. Of course, we weren't the only tourists returning from a disappointing evening out and we had some good company. We chatted for hours with fellow tourists. It turned out that peak season is great for meeting other tourists.

After Munich, our journey continued through the Austrian Alps, where my father's Peugeot 206 overheated on the Timmelsjoch High Alpine Road. After the car had cooled down at the summit of the mountain, we descended into Italy down a long and winding mountain road against the flow of cycling tourists climbing it. After a relaxing three-day break at the overcrowded Lake Garda, we continued our trip to Venice. We parked our car at Mestre, just before the long bridge into Venice, and travelled the last part by train. From an internet café in Bardolino, we had booked a small hotel just two days before our arrival. Our hotel - named Hotel dell'Opera - was probably our most expensive accommodation of the trip. We were there right at the peak of peak season: July 31 to August 2.

We did not like Venice at all. It was overcrowded. Back in 2010, buying advance tickets to museums and other tourist attractions was not possible yet. Most of our time was spent waiting in line for tourist attractions or walking slowing through the overpacked alleys of the beautiful city. All vaporetti, Venice's public transportation boats, were so full that we hardly understood how they kept afloat. Everything was expensive: our hotel, the food, and anything we tried to do. Our first impression of Venice was based on arguably the city's most horrible time. Peak season in Venice is probably the ugliest version of tourism you could find. Without any research, we struggled to find nice, affordable places to eat and we decided we just didn't like the city. Another lesson learned: if you travel to tourist hotspots during peak season, you better come prepared. It took us years to get back to Venice but when we did, we came prepared, and we have now fallen in love with the city.

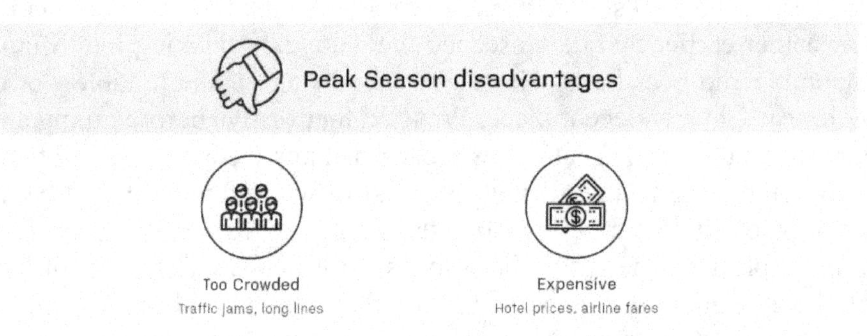

Peak season pricing

Venice, like any other tourist destination, is more expensive in peak season. It costs more money to get there, it costs more money to be there, and it even costs more money to get out. As with most other industries, pricing within the tourism industry is based on supply and demand. These basic economic laws influence not only pricing, but also whether a destination stays open or not in the slow season. As a profit-seeking industry, hotel owners and airlines will lower their prices if demand is low and there's a plentiful supply, since empty hotel beds and airline seats will cost the industry money and any they can fill will reduce their losses. Correspondingly, they'll increase their prices when demand is high or when supply is low. So for the travel industry, peak season is when most money is made. Demand surges while there is a limited supply of hotel rooms, restaurant seats, and tickets for entertainment. This means that peak season is not only the busiest time, it is also the most expensive time to travel. Outside peak season, the pendulum swings the other way. Demand drops while supply remains relatively stable, making it a cheaper time to travel.

Sometimes this price difference is clear, for example when you compare the price of hotel rooms. When it comes to other services, these price differences are a bit less obvious. Restaurants, for example, won't change their menu prices, but will offer you discounts or "tourist meals" during less busy periods that they will not offer you during peak season. Coupons and travel deals, such as all-inclusive packages, are often more expensive during peak season or not available at all. Outside peak season, tourists will benefit from lower prices as hotels need to compete in order to fill their beds and avoid having to pay their operating costs without guests.

The same holds true for the airline industry. Although it is generally more flexible in designating airplanes to varying destinations, supply and demand are also a major force in airline prices. During peak season, demand increases all across the world, meaning that all destinations become busier. Outside peak season, there are not that many destinations for airlines to allocate their excessive capacity to and so prices will drop outside the summer months. Not all airplanes can be allocated based on seasonality. Airlines also need to ensure they maintain their landing rights. To maintain those, they need to make use of their slots even if demand is low.

A relatively new phenomenon in the travel industry is dynamic pricing for tourist attractions. Although higher pricing in peak season is not new, the idea that these prices would change automatically from day to day is. Dynamic pricing is based on supply and demand as well. When more people want to visit certain attractions, the prices go up. If we take a theme park as an example, the price of a ticket will increase when more people want to visit the park and will drop when demand is low. Visiting a park on the weekend, when demand is higher for tourist attractions, will be more expensive than on normal weekdays. Even short-term changes like the weather can influence the price at which tickets are sold. For outdoor theme parks this means that the hot summer months are more attractive and therefore more expensive than others. Bank holidays and school vacations are other factors that will drive more people toward theme parks. All these factors will make demand go up while supply remains the same. Dynamic pricing allows tourist attractions to price their product accordingly. Of course, in peak season those prices will be higher on average than during low season.

Dynamic pricing is currently being rolled out to popular tourist attractions across the globe. GetYourGuide, a booking platform for experiences, is rolling out the technique at multiple attractions in Europe and the US. In an interview for Forbes.com[7], GetYourGuide's Chief Operating Officer Tao Tao explained to the magazine how dynamic pricing is being adopted by the Moulin Rouge in Paris. As an "early adopter" of automated dynamic pricing, the price of a seat at the venue depends on what show is on. "When the *Can Can* cabaret recommences, the price of a seat will depend on who's coming to dinner", Forbes writes.

While traveling outside peak season will save you serious money, not all types of vacation are possible outside peak season, since not all make sense without crowds. Party vacations to islands like Ibiza, Greek party towns, or Spain's Costa Brava are similar to spring break in the United States. Both spring break and the European equivalents need good weather and big crowds. Spring break without other spring breakers is not spring break.

It is also important to recognize that the ability to travel outside peak season is a luxury many people cannot afford. Those with children can only travel when their children are not in school, which means that families can only travel when other families can travel. Some European governments even take measures to ensure that the entire country isn't traveling at the same time. To mitigate the effect vacations have on infrastructure across Europe, countries like the Netherlands have been divided into multiple regions, each with a different beginning and end to the summer vacation. Other vacations, like autumn breaks or winter vacations, are scheduled on completely different weeks.

To conclude, what is better—peak season or low season— all comes down to what you prefer and when you are able to go on vacation. If you like full clubs, wild parties, big crowds and lots of people to meet and interact with, the peak season is most definitely your best option. If you have the choice, and you don't like full hotels or long lines at tourist attractions, anything but peak season is the best choice for you. But how can you travel outside of peak season and still enjoy your destination with great weather? To do that, you need to travel in the shoulder season.

Shoulder season

Our trip through Europe changed our perception of tourism. We still wanted to visit the world's most beloved destinations, but we were no longer willing to do so with more tourists than the destinations can bear. We therefore started to travel either to destinations that are less well-known or we travel outside peak season.

The world has changed rapidly since our trip to Munich, Austria, Lake Garda and Venice in 2010. More people than ever before are able to afford vacations and are traveling around the world. Technological changes resulted in greater mobility, while Airbnb shook up the hotel business. Add price-fighting airlines, Uber, e-scooters, commercial luggage storage, and hop-on hop-off buses to the mix and you have a travel revolution that has not only shaken up the travel industry itself but also the destinations and local communities that tourists visit. In the same way, the shoulder season is no longer what it used to be. As more people travel than ever before, more and more people are taking advantage of the slower seasons. Climate change is changing our travel patterns as well. Most destinations have become warmer and less rainy. While that's terrible for the environment, it also means that the shoulder season is now warmer than ever before which allows you to experience good weather in, for example, Venice as early as March and as late as October.

When is shoulder season?

The shoulder season is the travel season that sits between low and peak season. Just as we have two shoulders, there are also two different shoulder seasons: one that leads up to peak season and one that starts after peak season. This is usually spring and autumn. The two shoulder seasons are often referred to as either pre-season or late season. Since these are two distinctive seasons, we will use those terms to distinguish between the two.

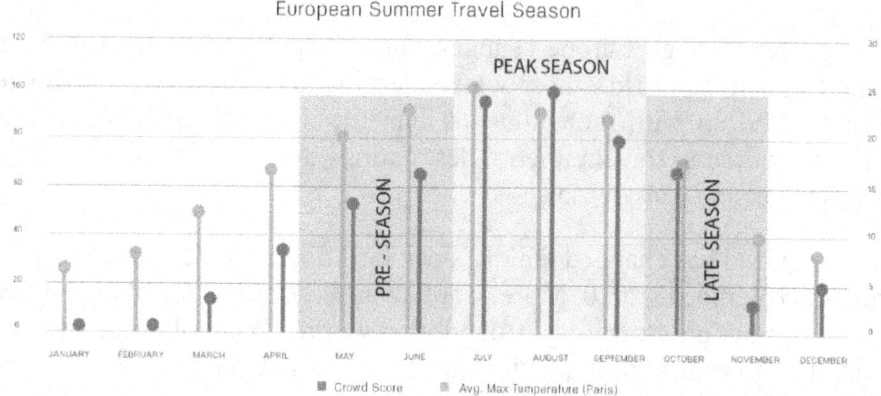

Figure 2: European summer travel seasons. SOURCES: Avoid-Crowds.com's average crowd score per month. Weather source is Google and is displayed in degrees Celsius.

Figure 4 visualizes the travel season in Paris. It is the same as Figure 1 but now also show both shoulder seasons. Paris has a typical season for a major European destination and serves as a perfect example for most parts of the continent. As the graph shows, the weather is best from June to August and those months are also the busiest months of the year as displayed with our crowd score. Although this graph is for Paris, it can be applied to basically all tourist destinations in the Northern Hemisphere. In the Southern Hemisphere, the travel season is reversed, peaking in December and January while the shoulder seasons trade places. The same happens for winter destinations. The ski season in the Alps starts in December and ends in April.

During both the pre-season and late season, tourist destinations are already attractive destinations. Most restaurants and bars will have opened and the seawater has usually has already warmed up to temperatures that allow for comfortable swimming. Hotels will have opened their outside hotel pools just like in peak season. Tourists can enjoy almost all of the same aspects of a good vacation during the shoulder season, but with one key difference: there are less tourists to compete with. There is no competition over sun beds in all-inclusive resorts, lines at tourist attractions are shorter, and prices will be lower. There are other advantages to traveling outside peak season, apart from having a quieter experience.

Figure 4 shows how the two shoulder seasons come just before and just after peak season. During these two seasons, you will be able to enjoy all the benefits of a vacation while not having to share it with unsustainably high number of fellow tourists. The two seasons are distinct and different, despite sharing the "shoulder season" name, and we will explore the pros and cons of traveling in both.

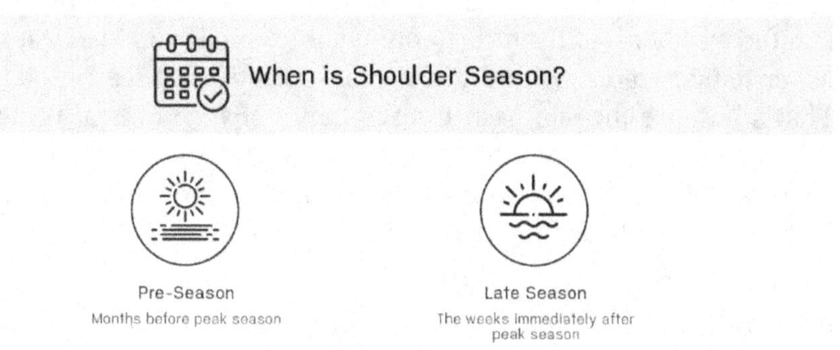

Pre-season

For most of Europe, as well as many destinations within the United States and Canada, the pre-season starts in mid-April. As weather conditions improve each week, so too does the size of the crowds at Europe's main tourist destinations. It will be especially busy around the Easter holidays. At Easter, almost the entire continent has a few days off and it can become very busy for the first time in the calendar year. This has a particular effect on larger cities and amusement parks, which see their first large crowds at this time. Meanwhile, many cruise ships will start to reposition from the Caribbean to the Mediterranean. This causes temporary surges in crowds at many coastal destinations. We will go into more detail about how to avoid large groups of cruise passengers later in this book.

Temperatures will be rising throughout pre-season, and in the future more and more hotel pools will be filled as tourists start to travel. Early pre-season, except for the Easter weekend, is noticeably less crowded than later in the season where we begin to approach peak season. For most destinations, May is a good month to travel. Although there are some bad weather days, temperatures are increasing rapidly by this time and rain clouds tend to stay away. The beginning of the month can be busy as some public holidays (Labor Day) and sporadic school vacations allow Europeans to travel. Other holidays that will make Europe feel extremely busy are Pentecost and Ascension Day. It is also wise to keep your eye on the events calendar for your chosen destination. While there's no sudden change in the number of tourists when pre-season transforms into peak season, crowds will rapidly grow from mid-June onwards as pre-season comes to an end.

The biggest benefit of pre-season is that it is arguably the slowest season, and weather conditions are usually good. But "usually good" means that the weather is still a little unpredictable, and if you like beach vacations, water temperatures will be lower than during peak season or late season. That's because the sun hasn't yet gotten a chance to heat up the sea. The average maximum water temperature in Mykonos, Greece is a chilly 18.1 degrees Celsius (59.5 Fahrenheit) in April, compared to a more comfortable 24.5 degrees Celsius (72.8 Fahrenheit) in September.

Late season

From the last weekend of August onwards, cities will gradually get quieter. Late season starts when most schools open their doors again in late August or early September and families are no longer able to travel. But while tourism slows down quickly, temperatures drop only gradually. This means that late season, especially September or early October, is still a very attractive time to travel.

Peak season is over, so there will be smaller crowds, and the weather is still fantastic. However, September is busier than it used to be in the past. It is the last good month to visit the Alps, Nordics, Baltics, or eastern Europe. For larger cities or the Mediterranean, early September can be just as busy as some weeks in August. Weekends in particular can be extremely crowded in larger European cities like Venice or Amsterdam.

Due to climate change, the late season is stretching out even longer. Where October used to be known for rain and cold weather, it is has now become a much warmer month with nicer temperatures than hot and steamy peak season months like July. Traveling in October is not (yet) very popular, but as more people realize how pleasant it is to travel with small crowds and decent enough weather, this is likely to change. If you're visiting a large city, where beach weather isn't a concern, October can be the perfect month to travel through Europe. Please be aware that school vacations in some countries, including Germany and the Netherlands, can make it busy from time to time. If you plan to travel in the second part of the late season, you should keep track of school vacations to make sure that you don't end up surrounded by families after all. Nevertheless, even during the busier October weeks, the crowds are far, far more manageable than during peak season.

How does the shoulder season impact you?

Once my wife and I finished university and started to work, our travel patterns shifted. We were no longer bound to travel within peak season when there were no classes to attend. In fact, many employers—including mine—encouraged those without children to travel outside peak season. That would spread out people taking days off over time, and our employer would not be left with only thinly spread staff when peak season came around.

In my early twenties, I would not have thought about taking a vacation outside peak season. Remember the trip down memory lane to Lloret de Mar? Party vacations without fellow tourists to party with was no vacation at all for the younger me. But once I started working, that changed. I now wanted to explore destinations around the world without the crowds. As we had learned on our trip through the heart of Europe, that means traveling outside the peak summer months of July and August.

One of the best shoulder season trips that we took, was when we went back to Venice in 2019. This time, we decided to travel to the Italian city in October. We had read multiple blogs that said that even in September, Venice could still be extremely crowded. Our data told us the same thing. Meanwhile, October weather in Venice is unpredictable but global warming has made the month warmer than ever before.

The benefits of traveling in the shoulder season became clear to us well before we even started the drive from our home in Austria – we had moved from the Netherlands to Austria by now. We normally decide when to travel based on whether we can get days off work to start with. But if those days are flexible, we look at two other things: the costs of traveling and the costs of staying at your destination. We traveled to Venice by car because we took our dog with us. Nevertheless, I checked flight prices and noticed that those were much cheaper than during peak season.

The real eye opener to us was the price of premium hotels. They appeared to be much more elastic than we thought, and the kind of prices offered in October in Venice were bargains compared to peak season. On the contrary, short-term rentals like Airbnb or those offered on Booking.com were still relatively expensive. One of the most attractive deals that we found was for the JW Marriott Venice. This luxury hotel is situated on a private island in the middle of the lagoon named by the hotel as "Isola delle Rose" or Rose Island, a good name for an island that does not have such a great history. It's an artificially created island that historically served as an hospital for people with contagious diseases and as an island for fuel storage before that. The hotel, however, is now a luxury oasis just a short boat ride away from the busy city. A rooftop swimming pool overlooks the Venetian lagoon and you have a view of Venice from some distance. In peak season, the most basic hotel rooms at the JW Marriott Venice sell for around EUR 400 per night. We got our room for EUR 224. But that was not all—we also received a free upgrade as part of our package, as well as a resort credit of EUR 50 per day. Taking that credit into account, our room effectively cost EUR 174, about a 60% discount on the price of the exact same room during peak season.

Not only was it cheaper to travel to Venice and stay there, there were many other benefits too. Normally the area between the Rialto Bridge and St. Mark's square is the busiest place in Venice. These two landmarks are only about 500 meters or a third of a mile from each other, but in peak season you need to schedule about half an hour to walk through the narrow alleys and crowded streets to get from one to the other. Without anyone on the streets, this walk would be about six minutes. Back on our trip as students in 2010, walking from Rialto Bridge to St. Mark's Square felt like taking a long city hike. In October, the streets were still far from empty but unlike early August, the crowds were manageable. The alleys between the bridge and square were not blocked. In August, window shopping tourists blocked the alleys, but in October, we were able to maneuver around those tourists easily, even with our dog.

In addition, there were no lines in October. If you visit Venice in August, you need to be ready to do some serious waiting. You have to stand in line to buy a ticket for public transport, you need to wait every time you want to get onto a vaporetto boat, and you need to battle to the exit when you want to get off. This is not the case in October. Of course, Venice remains a busy city, but the chaos of the summer is gone when the leaves turn brown. There are little to no lines at Venice's major tourist attractions and you can find a seat at any restaurant.

Of course, there are also some downsides to traveling in the shoulder season. We were extremely lucky during our trip to Venice in October as the weather was fabulous. We could even enjoy sunbathing and swimming in our hotel's rooftop pool. We recognize that this is not always the case. October weather in most of Europe is very unpredictable, and if you live far away from a destination, you can't wait until the last minute to ensure good weather before booking. Traveling in the second part of the late season in particular means that you need to be willing to take a risk with the weather. Furthermore, some services might scale down or close during the winter months. For us, the free shuttle boat to our hotel started operating a lighter schedule with fewer boats and although we didn't ever end up waiting in line, we did end up waiting once for a boat that didn't come at all.

Overall, traveling in the shoulder season has lots of benefits. If you have the choice and you're able to travel outside peak season, I would definitely recommend traveling in either the pre-season or late season. If you want to enjoy warm seawater, opt for the late season, and if you want to go on a city trip, May or October would both work well.

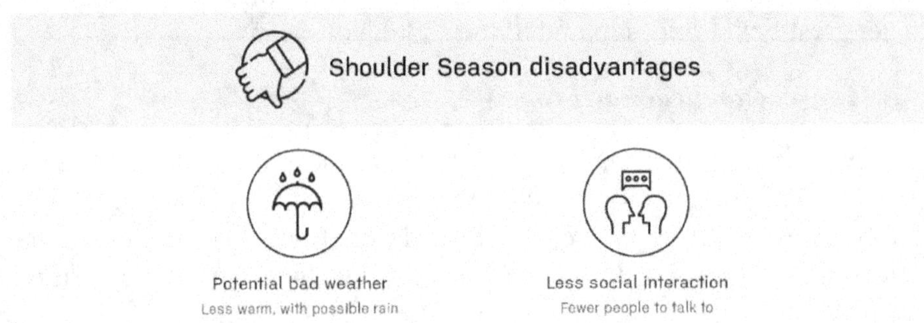

Benefits of traveling in the shoulder season

(Relatively) good weather

Of course, the weather is always unpredictable but global warming—while being devastating for the environment—does come with a perk for travelers; pleasant weather now lasts longer. But we recommend that before you decide on a trip somewhere in Europe in April or late October, you do your research first. Go online and find out what the climate for that particular destination is. When you do so, be aware that most climate models are based on the average weather over the last 30 years. With global warming, the weather is changing and has been much drier and warmer in recent years than most climate models will tell you. To get a more accurate impression of how the weather is likely to be, try to find the average weather for the last five years, rather than the last thirty.

Smaller crowds

Crowds are much smaller outside peak season. Although the shoulder seasons are becoming increasingly popular, they are still less crowded than in July or August. We really believe the shoulder season is the sweet spot; crowds are smaller and more manageable, but still big enough to keep the main attractions and tourist hotspots open as well as bars and restaurants.

Cheaper airfares

Airline tickets get a lot cheaper when there are fewer people competing for seats. As demand drops after the busy summer season, there aren't that many other destinations that airlines can send their planes to, which means that airlines have a much harder job trying to fill every seat. As a result, prices drop. If you are able to book far in advance, you are even more likely to get great ticket prices in one of the shoulder seasons.

More economical hotel rooms

Similar to airline tickets, hotel beds are more difficult to fill outside peak season. Demand drops while supply remains the same. Unlike airlines, hotels cannot simply move to other destinations that might be more attractive as the season ends. That's why hotels in many summer destinations will shut their doors in winter. The opposite is, of course, the case for winter sports resorts. Which is also why you will see many local governments and tourist boards trying to encourage tourists to visit those destinations outside the traditional season.

During the shoulder season, most hotels remain open but have to compete over fewer tourists. As a result, hotel owners will try to attract as many guests as possible by dropping room prices and making other offers available. As a tourist, this allows you to benefit from great deals like the one we got at the JW Marriott in Venice.

Lower prices for tourist attractions

Now that prices are published online rather than printed on a piece of paper that is valid for a full calendar year. Tourist attractions have the opportunity to price based on the actual demand there is, in the same way as airlines and hotels. That digitalization allows for automation of dynamic pricing and means that prices for tourist attractions go up when demand is high, and down when there is less demand. Although this is not yet common practice everywhere, it is most definitely the future, with US theme parks leading the way[8].

Disney World in Orlando for example doesn't change its prices during the day but has three different pricing seasons. The value season offers the lowest prices, followed by the slightly more expensive regular season, and the most expensive peak season. But even within those seasons, prices are different. Every calendar day seems to have its own price and the shoulder season is much more affordable than peak season.

Travel industry deals and promotions

Remember those hotels, airlines and tourist attractions that aren't able to sell all their seats, beds, or tickets outside peak season? Their owners will go to great lengths to sell as many as they can. Not only will these ownersreduce their price to get you to travel with them, but they'll compete in other ways as well. More than ever before, they will they try to tempt you to travel by offering discounts or additional perks. Hotels that only offer breakfast in peak season will start to offer all-inclusive packages in the shoulder season, including free food and drinks. Hotels will offer packages that include free access to museums or other local attractions. Local restaurants often partner up with hotels to offer a package of discounts. Promotions might even be offered by local governments.

In September 2019, I stayed in the Downtown Aloft hotel in Philadelphia. My booking at the hotel included a local promotion package that contained dinner vouchers, free museum access, and more. The JW Marriott on our trip to Venice threw in a 50 EUR resort credit per day. Those kind of deals are common when you travel outside peak season. It is a nice additional perk for not traveling with the masses.

Shoulder Season benefits

Less crowded
Things are calmer
outside peak season

OK weather
Less heat, chance
of rain

Less costly
Airline and hotel
prices drop

Low season

For some, traveling during low season may seem like an amazing opportunity. Sure, you get small crowds and little to no lines at tourist attractions, and airplane tickets usually cost close to nothing, with great deals for hotels. Unfortunately, it is low season for a reason. The single most important reason why it is low season is the weather.

My wife and I learned our lesson about low season the hard way. In December 2008, Mandy and I had been dating for little over six months. It was time for our first attempt at a vacation. As a Christmas gift, I wanted to surprise her with a weekend city break in Europe. A romantic weekend trip to Milan sounded absolutely perfect and after some online research, a Ryanair flight to Bergamo—a town north of Milan—caught my eye. The tickets for both of us cost EUR 40 return and an additional EUR 20 to pay by credit card, which was basically the only option available, so for EUR 30 per person, Mandy and I had a return ticket from Eindhoven Airport to Bergamo.

Low Season benefits

No Crowds
Things are calmer
outside peak season

Cheap
Airline and hotel prices
are low

When we arrived at Bergamo airport on January 14 2009, it was covered in snow. Unlike the towns further north, which are situated in the Alps and used to snow, the city of Milan does not handle cold weather too well. Traffic struggled, visibility was poor, and pathways were blocked. From Bergamo, we had to take a bus to downtown Milan. The bus ride took a little over an hour with the extra traffic caused by the snow.

Thank goodness we were young and in love, because our experience in Milan was pretty terrible. Public transport wasn't operating normally, and pathways were blocked by huge piles of snow that built up as snow shufflers cleared the road for cars by dumping it onto the sidewalk. It was freezing cold, and when the temperature did eventually start to improve, the big piles of snow turned into messy piles of brown slush. I guess we could simply have been unlucky. The weather in Milan in January can be much better than it was when we experienced it.

Back then, Ronaldinho, David Beckham, and Clarence Seedorf were international stars playing for AC Milan. As it was winter, the closest thing I could get to a football match was a tour of San Siro, the home stadium of both AC Milan and Internatizionale. It was a group tour through the football temple that was built for the 1990 FIFA World Cup. Given the popularity of the team, filled as it was with international superstars, the stadium tour was popular. Even on a snow-covered January day, there were still enough people to keep the tours going. But the tour group was small, which meant everyone had plenty of opportunity to ask questions and we could see a little more and a little better than you would during peak season.

More relevant for my not-so-much-of-a-football-fan wife, there was no line to see Da Vinci's famous Last Supper mural. In fact, there were no lines at any of Milan's tourist attractions. The city was almost deserted. But with the ugly weather and city's inability to properly clear the snow, I understood perfectly well why it was so cheap to get to Milan. There was no tourist reason for us to be there in the darkest days of winter. It was slow season for a reason.

 **Low Season disadvantages**

Potential bad weather

Less warm, with possible rain

Less social interaction

Traveling like a lone wolf

Low season can be busy too

While the regular low season runs from November to May, there are some short but seriously crowded weekends or days you need to know about. During the low season, we see some of the busiest individual days and weeks of the year. These days are unusual peaks that surround the world's most well-known national holidays.

Christmas

Airline tickets and hotel room prices surge around Christmas. Not only are expats and business travelers returning to their families, but many people will go on vacation during the Christmas break and around New Year's Eve. This once again has to do with school holidays and the ability of families with children to travel again. That has an effect on winter sports resorts and cities alike as large crowds are attracted by Christmas activities.

The Christmas effect can be felt as early as late November. Cities known to be "Christmas destinations" become especially crowded. Think about cities like London or New York where lots of tourists will do their Christmas shopping on their visit. In Europe, Christmas markets have become increasingly popular over the last decades, with destinations in Germany and Austria becoming more crowded each year.

New Year's Eve is another crowded night with most hotel beds in major destinations occupied. Collectively counting down for the New Year has become a major tradition that seems to attract lots of young travelers, including the author of this book. My wife and I are among many who travel for a unique New Year's Eve experience. We have seen the ball drop in

Times Square, were part of crazy New Year's nights in Amsterdam, an amazing experience in Kuala Lumpur, but also more conservative partying in Salzburg. One of the weirdest New Year's Eve experiences I had was in Shanghai before I met Mandy, where only the expats and tourists seemed to care about the change of calendar year as the true experience for locals would be Chinese New Year happening a few months later.

Easter, Pentecost, Whit Monday

Easter marks the start of the regular tourist season in many European destinations. Around the Christian holiday, schools across the European continent will get one or more weeks off. That means Europeans once again have the opportunity to travel. With fewer and fewer Europeans spending the religious holiday in church, they're much more likely to travel instead. The same happens during Pentecost, Whit Monday and many other traditionally religious public holidays.

The travel appetite combined with the potential for good weather results in sudden peaks in travel. This peak is especially noticeable in theme parks, major tourist attractions like the Eiffel Tower, and in the historic city centers of the European continent. At Avoid Crowds, we keep track of all these religious holidays and add them to our data model.

Other local and national holidays

King's Day in Amsterdam is a one-day celebration of the birthday of the Dutch monarch. The entire country comes to a halt and dresses up in orange, but it is Amsterdam where the celebrations are the most enthusiastic. All the streets are packed, there's not a single hotel bed available, and the canals are full of boats. In other words, on this low season April day in Amsterdam suddenly sees one of the most crowded days of the year.

There are many more national or local public holidays similar to King's Day that come with major crowds. Labor Day in many European countries take place on May 1, and often leads to protests or even riots in many of Europe's cities. In France in particular, Labor Day is not a good day for a trip to the French capital. It is always worth doing a bit of research to see when any national holidays are and why it can get busy at your destination.

WHAT CAUSES CROWDS?

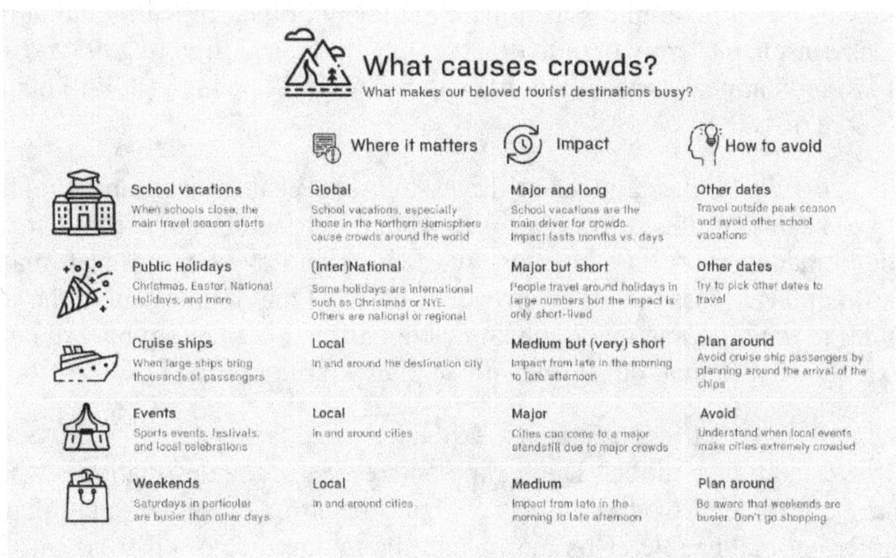

While we knew early on that school vacations were key to building a solid data model for predicting crowds, there was much more research that needed to be done to refine it. School vacations only tell us a part of the story on why it is busy. They don't explain the sudden peaks in tourists caused by, for example, public holidays or local events. We understood that we needed to gather lots of other data to ensure we have all the building blocks to predict crowds on any given day in any city.

That we needed to do more was also made clear to us in the feedback we received on our website. Although many travelers found our crowd predictions useful, the score wasn't very helpful in distinguishing between extremely busy days and "normal" peak season days. A discussion on Tripadvisor[9], pointing out our weaknesses, made us see that we needed to make some adjustments. A user, pretty much said he wouldn't use Avoid Crowds because he wanted to know which days in August were unbearable and which ones were OK. At that time our website could not answer this question but we had all the data to improve.

So we went to work and made some changes. Our crowd prediction score was great at telling you when it was peak season. But, like the person on Tripadvisor, most users already know which months will be busy. So we made sure our website will not only show you when it is peak season, but will also differentiate between regular peak season and those horrible super busy days. For example: when there are many cruise ships in town during peak season, our crowd predictions score will be very high (e.g. 95-100). If it is a regular peak season day, the number will still be high (80-90) but not a score of 100.

To fully understand what drives tourism, peak season and shoulder season aside, we need to investigate what other factors impact tourism. In the remainder of this chapter, we will explore exactly what makes destinations across the globe crowded and what that tells us about the best times to travel. Armed with the knowledge from this chapter you will know exactly what to look out for when you plan your next trip.

All the metrics or events explained here are part of the Avoid-Crowds.com data model. Depending on the size of the destination—which can be measured by the number of hotel beds for example—they play a larger or smaller role. This means that the importance of all these metrics very per destination. A single large cruise ship that arrives in Miami has a relatively small impact on how busy the South Florida city becomes compared to the impact of the same ship on small islands in the Mediterranean or Caribbean.

School vacations

As explained in other chapters, school vacations are the most important metric when you predict tourist crowds. There are the only times that most families, and those in college, can leave their homes and go on a vacation. But are some school vacations more important than others? We already know that domestic tourism is the biggest contributor to overall tourism, so the timing of domestic school vacations is the number one factor we have to take into consideration. The second most important metric is the timing of international school vacations and the impact those have on tourist departures.

There are so many different school vacations throughout the world and it's important to take demographics into consideration. Summer school vacation in Luxembourg, with a total population of 626,000, will hardly have an impact on tourism to the larger countries that surround it. Tourism from Germany, however, with a population of 83 million, has a major impact on the entire European continent. With most tourists either traveling within their own country or within the EU, there are only a handful of countries that you need to take into consideration when looking at travel to Europe.

Generally speaking, when you want to know how crowded a destination can become, you look at the host country and those countries in Europe that have the most tourists that travel internationally: Germany, the United Kingdom, Russia, Italy, France, and the Netherlands[10].

Country	International Tourists – Number of Departures 2018
China	149 Million
Germany	108 Million
United States	93 Million
Hong Kong SAR, China	92 Million
United Kingdom	70 Million
Russian Federation	42 Million
Italy	33 Million

Figure 5: Tourist departures by country. SOURCE: World Bank under CC BY-4.0 license.

As Figure 5 shows, the country with the most internationally departing tourists in the world is China, but not all of those tourists find their way to Europe. The same holds true for citizens from the United States and Hong Kong, who together with Germany and the United Kingdom make up the nations with the most travelers in the world. Interestingly, some of the countries on the list have more international departures than they have citizens. Germany, with a population of 83 million, has 108 million international departures, meaning that on average each German citizen takes 1.3 international trips, including business trips.

The most important school vacation to take into consideration in terms of the time of year is the summer break. Most European and US schools will close their doors for over a month. In some parts of Europe, especially in the south of the continent, this vacation can last up to two months.

Public holidays

Public holidays, especially when they fall on days with favorable weather, cause major but short-lived peaks in global travel. Public holidays usually mean that children don't have to go to school and families are able to go on a short vacation. This short window of opportunity to travel leads to increased international travel, but also causes a surge in people traveling within their own country. The number of day trips, where people are a tourist for a single day without staying away overnight, increase massively when people get a day off work and, on public holidays, entire countries get the opportunity to be a day-tripper.

Public holidays have a major impact on cities. Popular city destinations in Europe such as Paris, Venice, Rome, and Amsterdam get extremely crowded. Those living in the city don't have to go to work and can explore parks and attractions near their home. Those living an acceptable distance from tourist attractions will hop in their car and go to the beach, city, or to tourist attraction they normally wouldn't have time for. Public holidays are the busiest days of the year for theme parks and museums, and when the weather is good that effect extends to parks, beaches and lakes.

The most important holidays

Month	Europe	USA	Other Countries
January	Jan 1: New Year's Day Epipany	New Year's Day Martin Luther King Jr. Day	New Year's Day Orthodox Christmas Australian Day (AUS) Republic Day (IND)
Feburary	Carnival		Chinese New Year (CHN) Carnival (BRA)
March			
April	Easter Liberation Day (ITA)		Easter
May	Labor Day Bank Holidays (CBR) Ascension Day Victory in Europe Day (FRA)	Memorial Day	Labor Day Eid- al- Fitr Golden Week (JPN)
June	Whit Monday Republic Day (ITA)		Victory Day (RUS) Russia Day (RUS)
July	Jul 14: Bastille Day (FRA)	Jul 4: Independence Day (USA)	
August			Independence Day (IND)
September		Labor Day	
October	Oct 3: Unity Day (GER)		National Day (CHN) Golden Week (CHN)
November		Veterans Day Thanksgiving	Unity Day (RUS)
December	Dec 25/26: Christmas Dec 31: New Year's Eve	Dec 25/26: Christmas Dec 31: New Year's Eve	Dec 25/26: Christmas Dec 31: New Year's Eve

Figure 6: Public holidays in Europe, the US, and other countries. Dates of religious holidays may vary each year. Various sources.

Figure 6 shows the most important public holidays in the United States, Europe, and other countries that can have a serious impact on global travel such as China, India and Russia. For some of these public holidays, such as

Independence Day or Christmas, the dates are fixed, meaning they fall on the same day each year. Other public holidays, such as Easter or Labor Day, fall on different dates each year. You can find an overview of the specific dates for each of these holidays on our website.

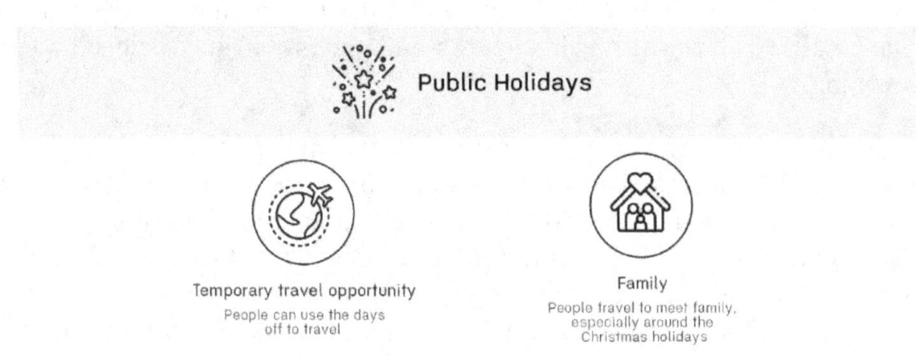

Cruise ship schedules

Although the increase in tourists caused by the arrival of a cruise ship is short-lived and highly localized, the impact can be serious. When we look at our data, cruise ship arrivals need to be divided into two categories, the first being destinations where passengers start and end their cruises. In these destinations, cruise ship passengers will usually book a few nights in an hotel near the port from which their ship departs. The often-heard criticism that cruise passengers don't spend any money in the cities they visit is not true for many these beginning and end destinations. These cruise passengers book hotels, buy meals in restaurants, and can have a positive effect on the local economy with their stay. The situation is different, however, for those destinations that are on the itinerary of the cruise ship after it leaves its initial port, which are often not equipped to handle a sudden surge in tourists.

Imagine visiting a small coastal town in the Mediterranean or Caribbean. The blue waves break on the rocky shores as you walk through narrow streets and bask in the sun. While you enjoy breakfast outside your hotel or at a local restaurant, you notice that something is going on in the town's port. A massive cruise ship with a capacity of over 6,000 is unloading cruise passengers into the town. The cruise passengers can leave their ships in the morning, usually around 8 or 9 a.m., and need to be back in the afternoon at around 4 or 5 p.m. That gives them about eight hours to walk through your peaceful, cozy, vacation destination. For those eight hours, the situation completely changes. Roads around the port will get congested, restaurants and bars will fill up, and tour groups will dominate the local landmarks. Your peace and quiet is over until it's time for the cruise passengers to return to their ships in the afternoon. By the time things have calmed down again, landmarks and shops will have closed for the evening.

The serious impact cruise travel can have on destinations is as gigantic as the ships themselves have become over the years. Global cruise capacity—the total number of passengers that the world's cruise ships can carry collectively—has been rapidly increasing over the last ten years. In total, there are about 25 million cruise passengers per year. That's the equivalent of the combined population of the Netherlands and Austria, or of Florida and Louisiana.

Needless to say, some destinations are completely overrun by cruise passengers. Cozumel in Mexico, an island with a population of 100,000, welcomes up to 4.3 million cruise passengers per year based on our own calculations. If these cruise passengers were evenly spread over the year, Cozumel sees around 11,780 passengers per day, almost 12% of the local population. That might sound just about manageable, but the problem is that these cruise passengers are not evenly spread over the year. There are some days with eight or more cruise ships in port, bringing over 35,000 cruise passengers to the island. Imagine trying to plan a nice, relaxing excursion on that day.

If you're in a destination that's relatively small but that attracts a lot of cruise ships, it is smart to keep track of when they arrive and depart. You can plan ahead, for example by not visiting certain landmarks during the hours that these ships are in port. It might also be wise to avoid the area near the port at those times as you will almost certainly end up in a traffic jam. If you're at a port where passengers start and end their cruise, the situation gets even worse as you can expect double the number of passengers in port that day.

Probably one of the most well-known places to be negatively affected by the global surge in cruise traffic is Venice in Italy. The beautiful city no longer hosts the world's largest ships, but still bears the brunt of overtourism caused by the global cruise industry. Without COVID-19, the city would have seen 56 large cruise ships arriving and departing in port 514 times throughout the year. In total these 514 arrivals would bring up to 1.23 million cruise passengers to the city if the ships sail at full capacity. We published that number in February 2020, based on the data we gather ourselves, and a local Venetian newspaper picked up our blog and ran the story. The number was disputed by Venice's port authorities who only provide numbers for actual arrivals after the end of the year.

Like many other places, cruise ship arrivals in Venice are not evenly spread throughout the year. In fact, most cruise ships arrive in the lagoon when there are already lots of other ships in town. The negative effect cruise ships can have when it comes to overtourism is made worse by incredibly bad planning. We discovered an interesting but shocking pattern in Venice cruise ship schedule. Unlike other cities, cruise ship arrivals in Venice are not evenly spread across days of the week and most cruise ships tend to arrive in Venice during already busy weekends.

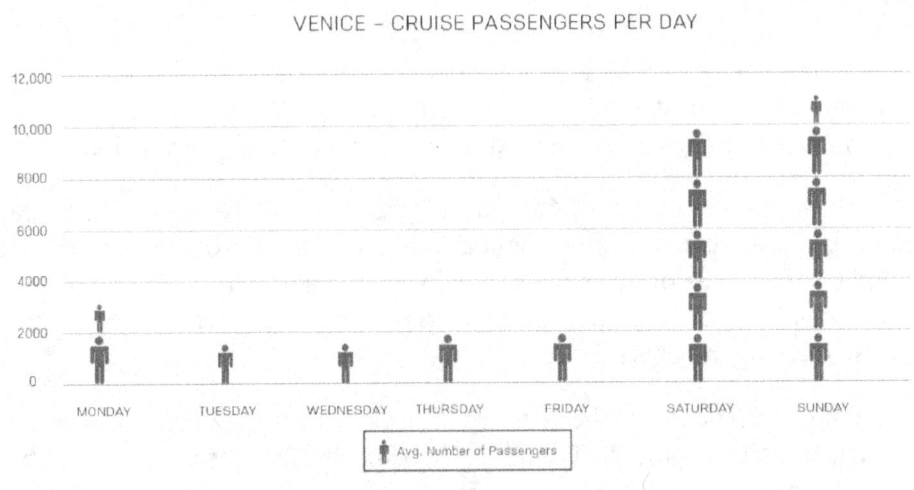

Figure 7: Cruise passengers in Venice by day of the week. SOURCE: Avoid-Crowds.com

Looking at ships that carry 500 passengers or more, Venice welcomed slightly over 1 million cruise passengers in 2019. On average, that's around 6,400 passengers per day but as Figure 7 shows, passengers aren't spread evenly spread out through the week and during the already busy weekends, the number of cruise passengers in Venice increases massively. An average of 1,685 visitors on a Wednesday is in stark contrast to a shocking ~10,000 more on a Sunday, when the city greets an average of 11,621 passengers.

If we take this weekend rush into consideration, we can clearly see that the average number of cruise ship passengers is actually relatively low on weekdays. Monday through Friday, the average number of cruise visitors drops to a low of 2,658. What a difference.

Furthermore, the city is better equipped to absorb large numbers of cruise passengers on weekdays, much more so than the weekend, since day-trippers and city trippers are usually more likely to plan their trip for the weekend too—although this effect is not as clear during peak season.

Venice's peak season is long, but if we take the busiest months of the year—July and August—Venice's cruise ship problem gets worse. The average number of daily cruise ship passengers over these two months increases from 6,400 to 7,268. As a result, Venice jumps closer to the top of the list of **Europe's busiest cruise destinations**: from 9th place to 5th place.

When you only look at weekend arrivals in those two months, Venice becomes the busiest cruise port in Europe, overtaking some of its best-equipped and busiest ports, including Barcelona and Civitavecchia.

With an average of 14,453 passengers each Sunday and 12,815 each Saturday, it is easy to see that Venice has a scheduling problem. The average number of arrivals on weekdays remains stable and hardly diverts from the yearly average; even in peak season, Venice only sees an average of 2,869 cruise passengers on weekdays.

The busiest days of the year are in peak season. In 2019, the worst day to visit Venice was the **28th of July** when six cruise ships with a capacity of over 2,500 passengers or more were in Venice and European schools had just started their vacations. It created a toxic overtourism cocktail made up of weekend day-trippers, Europeans on vacation, and six of the world's largest cruise ships.

The cruise season peaks when tourism peaks in the area. For the Caribbean, that means mid-December to February while for the Mediterranean and other European cruise destinations it is June to September. But you cannot expect zero cruise passengers outside these busy months. The cruise season is getting longer and longer; Venice sees some of its busiest cruise days as late as October. For tourists expecting a low season day in Venice, a bad day in October might be a rude awakening.

Although it's becoming increasingly difficult to completely avoid cruise ship tourism, it is very easy to be informed about the situation at your destination. You can simply search for cruise ship schedules on Google. Type in "cruise ship schedule [Dubrovnik/Nassau/other destination]". There are multiple websites to choose from that show you what ships are in port on what day. Some even add the number of cruise passengers based on the capacity of the ship.

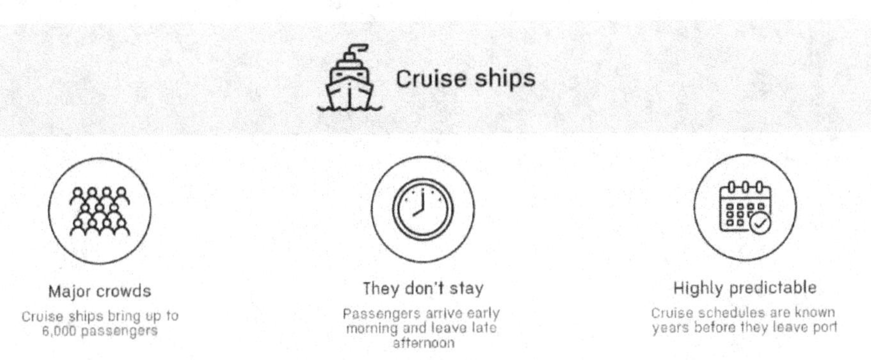

Local events

There's nothing that attracts larger crowds than big local events. Marathons, pop concerts, sports games and large fairs can quickly fill up hotel rooms and streets. Think about the Super Bowl or the World Cup Final. Football fans will take over everything. Hotel rooms on the night of the game will become scarce and the prices for those available are sky high.

Local events filling up all available hotel beds is what allegedly led to the foundation of Airbnb back in 2007. When Airbnb founders Brian Chesky and Joe Gebbia noticed that all the hotels in San Francisco were fully booked during the local Industrial Design Conference they bought air beds and rented them out online as "Air Bed and Breakfast". After successfully renting out the air beds, they launched Airbnb just before the

2008 Democratic National Convention in Denver, where over 600 people stayed in their accommodation.

Although it took Airbnb a few years to fully get off the ground, the inspiration came out of the lack of available hotel beds during peak demand. Conventions, congresses, sports events, and many other types of large events will disrupt the local dynamic of supply and demand for a short period of time. And this short disruption is not limited to the number of available hotel beds. Streets will fill up quickly, bars and restaurants will be full, and it's not the most pleasant or most relaxing time to be in town as a tourist. The disruption effect of each of these types of event is different so we decided to list each separately.

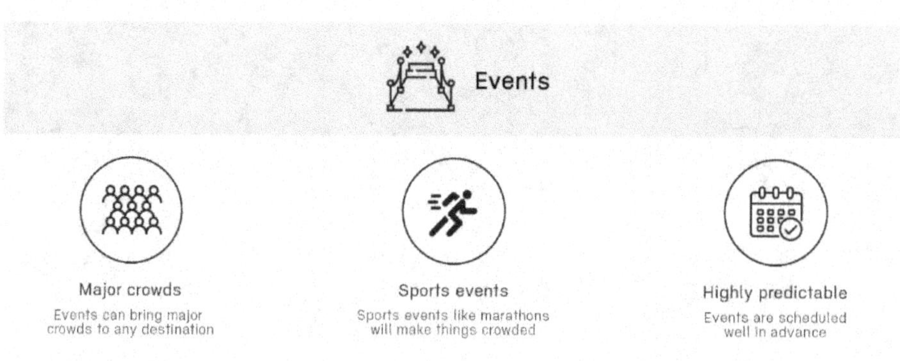

Political events and protests

Political events often come with protests, and a major protest can ruin a vacation. When your hotel is situated in the middle of a street that is filled with protestors, police, and tear gas, you will not be able to enjoy your valuable vacation days. Although protests are not generally predictable, some can be predicted. Political rallies are usually a reliable indicator of potential unrest. Elections too are worth avoiding if you can.

In France, there is even a national holiday that sparks riots year after year. On May 1, it's Labor Day in most of Europe. Even in the middle of the COVID-19 lockdown, protests rocked cities across Europe. In Paris, masked protestors clashed with riot police in the city center. This is a recurring annual 'event' that could lead to road closures, a large police presence, and violence. Although protests occur across Europe on this day, Franceis particular affected.

You can avoid potential hotspots by doing your research. If there is political unrest or protests in a city you wanted to visit, adjusting your plans is the most sensible thing to do. While staying clear from riots or unrest will most likely keep you safe, it's better to be safe than sorry. Even if that costs a little more money, it is worth it. If you happen to be on vacation already when a city is struck by riots, keep calm. Find alternative things to do, or leave. Follow the instructions of local authorities or your embassy, and ask your hotel for tips.

Political events like protests can disrupt your vacation. I took this image in London in 2019, as protestors for and against Brexit gathered around parliament.

Sports

There are two categories of sporting events: participatory events like marathons where the public can participate in the event themselves and spectator events where people come to watch professional athletes compete against each other. Spectator events include football, both American and European, as well as motor racing or road bike racing.

Participatory sports events

Participatory sports events are among the most disruptive events a city can host. They are mostly held on the weekend, so that they do not disrupt the local economy and way of living too much. The absolute champion of disruptive participatory sports is the marathon, which almost every city on our planet now hosts, notably New York, London, Paris and Rome. Major streets in cities will be closed off, tens of thousands of runners will book hotel rooms, and large numbers of spectators add to the crowds.

Spectator sports events

The Super Bowl or the Champions League Final are two examples of annual sports events that can make cities in Europe and the United States extremely crowded. European Club Football can lead to some of the continent's most famous tourist destinations becoming unexpectedly and unseasonably crowded.

International football competitions, such as the World Cup or UEFA European Championships, can have a similar effect with even more international fans showing up. Even those without tickets to the event will likely watch on the streets which can lead to major traffic blockades and parts of cities being sealed off. Traffic jams around the stadium, fan marches, and fully crowded city centers are to be expected. If you have to catch a flight or train, it is vital to take this into consideration, leave earlier or go on foot.

Many European football clubs have a very loyal following of fans that travel internationally with their club. These fans are not always well behaved and can cause major police presence and disruptions. Most European clubs don't have problems with hooligans anymore, but each year some riots still erupt. Simply staying away from the fans of the visiting club and the area around the stadium will keep you safe. And don't wear a football jersey around fans of the opposing team. Wearing the jersey from a rival team, even when they aren't playing, could get you into uncomfortable situations.

To keep order during high risk games, local authorities can put emergency regulations in place. These might include a temporary ban on alcohol in some parts of the city or random searches of people in certain areas. Some fan groups march from the city center to the stadium, and it's smart to keep away from this too.

So how can you know when to expect football or other sports events hitting town? It requires a bit of research. Search for the local clubs and the dates you plan to travel. European club football always takes place from Tuesday to Thursday evening from September to early December and continues with play offs from February to early May. American sports are spread over the calendar year, but generally bring less disruption to cities.

Other major disruptive sports events include Formula 1 city races, like the Monte Carlo Grand Prix, Tennis Grand Slams or the Tour de France finish in Paris. All these events can take one or multiple days and it is goo to find out what is happening during your stay so you can make sure you can enjoy your stay as planned.

Weekends

Remember the importance of people having the opportunity to travel in causing crowds? Schools aren't open on Saturday or Sunday and most employees don't have to work on the weekends either. That makes weekends perfect for day trips, weekend trips, and even long weekend vacations when you add one or two paid vacation days on top. As a result, weekends are more crowded than weekdays, even in the most touristic areas that attract the majority of international tourists. Not only will more people be traveling, but those living in the cities you are visiting as a tourist will be free to enjoy what the city has to offer. such as shopping or visiting museums, zoos and other tourist attractions.

When you are able to travel during the week, or add a couple of weekdays to your weekend break, we would recommend avoiding the busiest areas on the weekend. Save the tourist attractions for the weekdays and try to find less touristy things to do on the weekend. If you are completely free to choose, we would recommend traveling outside the weekend altogether, when tourist destinations are less crowded.

There is one caveat to this general rule. Destinations that attract lots of business travelers, such as downtown Manhattan or the City of London, might *actually* be less crowded on the weekend. As a result, hotels are more economically affordable as hotels try to bring in tourists to replace those on business trips who are vacating their rooms. Each destination is different, and within each destination, there are even more differences between areas. Doing your research before your book might save you money, and will most certainly help you avoid the crowds.

OVERTOURISM

When my mother visited the Leaning Tower of Pisa in 1965, you could drive your car onto the streets of Pisa and park right in the complex that houses the tower. After parking her car, she could walk onto the grass of the complex and freely explore the area. My mother recently sent an old black and white photo of the visit and there are hardly any other tourists to be seen. It's a stark contrast to now, 55 years later. Pisa has changed. The Italian city is completely overrun by tourists. There are so many who want to visit the Leaning Tower of Pisa, in fact, tourists can't take their cars into the city. Cars have been banned from the city and strict rules are in place to ensure that tourism has the least possible impact on the people who live there.

Behavioral science research[11] has shown that spending money on new experiences yields more happiness than spending it on new products. This might explain why people love to travel so much and why we are now moving around more than ever before. The focus of this book is not on why we travel, but the fact is that we do it more than ever before, and as soon as the pandemic is behind us, travel is likely to continue to grow. While tourism has been growing rapidly over the last few decades, this growth really started to pick up in the last fifteen years. Since 2008, the total number of tourist departures has doubled.

Unfortunately, that growth in tourism has some serious consequences for the destinations we visit. Mass tourism might not be new, but over the last decades it has developed into a really ugly beast. With too many people traveling to locations that are not able to handle the levelof tourism we see today, things have become unsustainable. Now, instead of tourists being merely visitors at their destinations, they are changing them, mostly for the worse rather than for the better.

While all that traveling has brought wealth and jobs to some parts of the world, in other places it has become too much. As local inhabitants are forced out of their houses due to rising real estate prices, tourism is destroying the livability of whole cities and rural areas. When tourism has a negative impact on local communities or ruins the experience of tourists, it is called "overtourism".

Overtourism is, by itself, a phenomenon that might be difficult to define in exact terms, but it essentially describes the negative effects of having too many tourists in one place at the same time. When you visit cities like Paris, Rome, or Venice you are likely to experience the effects of overtourism first hand. In these cities, the amount of tourists can be overwhelming and it feels like it has taken over normal life. You can't find a grocery store and 90% of the people you bump into are other tourists. The infrastructure is not designed for this kind of tourism flows and there are inevitable consequences.

The World Tourism Organization[12] describes the term well: Overtourism occurs in "destinations where hosts or guests, locals or visitors, feel that there are too many visitors and that the quality of life in the area or the quality of the experience has deteriorated unacceptably. It is the opposite of Responsible Tourism which is about using tourism to make better places to live in and better places to visit. Often both visitors and guests experience the deterioration concurrently".

Overtourism is the name of the disease, but it is the symptoms of the disease from which we suffer.

What causes overtourism?

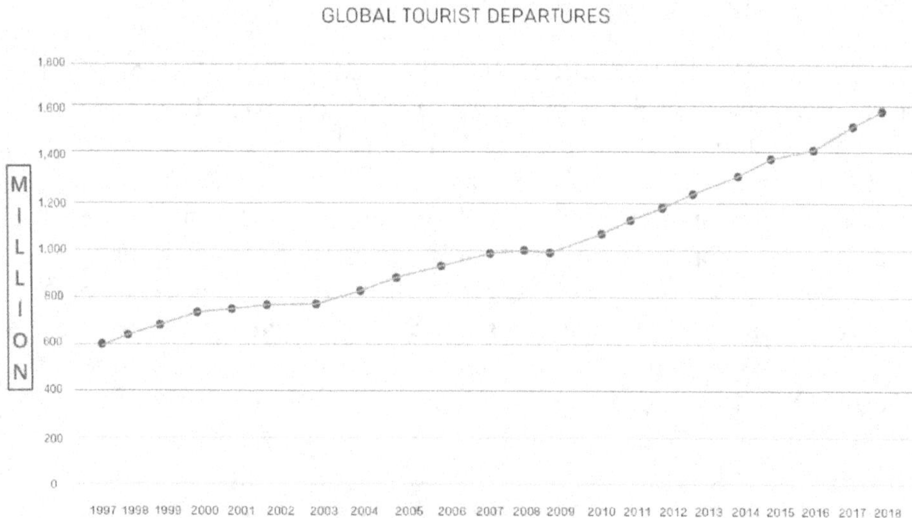

Figure 8: Growth in global international tourist departures. SOURCE: World Bank under CC BY-4.0 license.

Before we describe some of the most annoying symptoms of overtourism, we need to understand what causes the disease. Why is tourism growing so quickly?

The first cause of overtourism is obvious: it's not just the number of tourists that's rising, it's the number of people. We live in an increasingly populated world. Since my mother traveled to Italy in the 1960s, our planet's population has almost tripled from three billion to around eight billion in 2020[13].

Another factor that contributes to increasing numbers of tourism is the falling cost of travel. Back in the 1960s, airline tickets were expensive and the general population had less disposable income to buy those expensive tickets. In 2020, that situation has changed. In most developed countries, we now have more disposable income than 30 years ago. At least some of that disposable income is spent on vacations. A US study shows that "travel and tourism" is a major consumer spending priority, with leisure travel as a budget priority for 70.6% Americans. Only a small portion of Americans

(6.1%) give travel a low priority[14]. Similar trends occur in high income countries all over the world. While back in 1965, when my mother visited Pisa, travel was a luxury only a few could afford, now many households can afford multiple vacations per year.

Meanwhile, citizens of countries that had limited travel opportunities in the past also now have increasing access to travel. The most striking example is China. The number of international departures from China back in 2010 was about 10.5 million. Since 2010, tourism departures from the world's most populated country have seen exponential growth. In 2018, the World Bank recorded almost 150 million departures from China, a growth of more than 1,400% in just 8 years. The second most populated country in the world, India, is not showing similar exponential growth—at least not yet—but has seen international tourism departures increase by 600% since 2000, when only about 4.4 million departures were recorded.

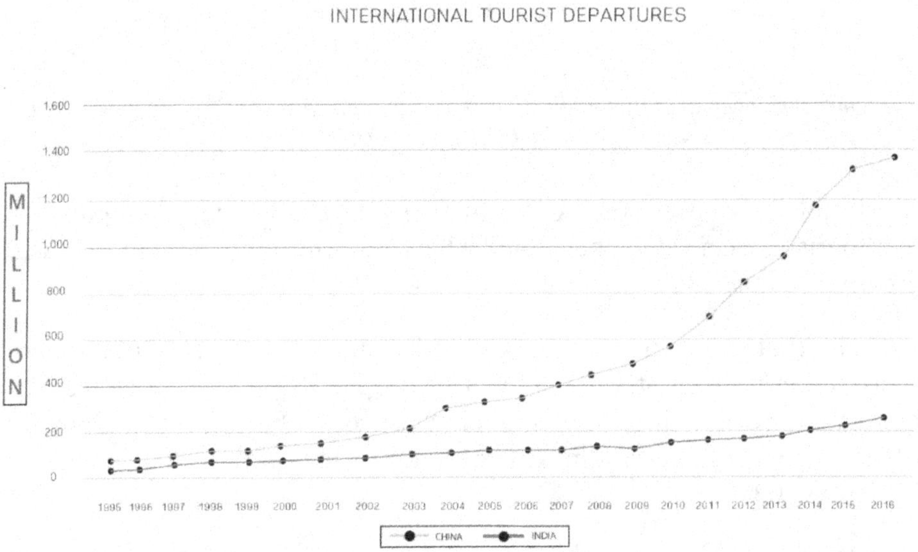

Figure 9: Growth in international tourist departures from India and China. SOURCE: World Bank under CC BY-4.0 license.

With a rising world population, a major increase in disposable income, and countries emerging as new sources of tourism, more people are able to travel than ever beforeBut unfortunately, this simple rise in the number of tourists does not tell the whole story. There is another factor that has not been extensively researched nor described.

Important to understand is that most tourists never leave their country[15]. The 1.6 billion international departures shown in Figures 8 and 9 come on top of the biggest contributor to mass tourism: domestic tourism. That means on top of Italians staying in Italy and Americans not traveling outside the United States. Although there are no exact numbers, a study from 2005 showed that the number of domestic tourists outnumber international departures by 5 to 1[16].

Even with huge numbers of tourists hopping on airplanes and crossing borders, the world could probably handle many more than we have now in different circumstances. The sheer number of tourists is not our biggest problem. The most important problem that we have is that the huge numbers of tourists are all interested in visiting exactly the same places.

Somehow, we all seem to share the same travel bucket list: The Great Wall of China, Machu Picchu, Barcelona, Venice, the Mona Lisa, Hallstatt, Amsterdam, New York City, Rome, and many other locations around the world. No matter how many more people are able to and interested in traveling, we can't expand the size of these destinations or add new destinations for them to visit. It simply gets more crowded in the places that are already crowded. While these destinations are heavily impacted by tourism, villages and cities as little as five kilometers (three miles) away from these hotspots often have no tourists at all. Mass tourism is hyperlocal and hyper focused.

That is why governments in places that suffer from overtourism, are trying to spread tourists out geographically. By making other areas outside the main destination more attractive to tourists, governments are trying to lure tourists away from the most crowded places so that the economic benefits that come with tourism are also more evenly spread. Another way of spreading tourists out is by trying to promote travel when a destination is not usually as busy, such as the low season. Venice even goes so far as to discourage people from coming on the busiest days through their own online crowd prediction tool.

It doesn't stop in our cities. Not even the most isolated parts of our planet seem to be immune to overtourism. In 2019, pictures of the summit of Mount Everest shocked the world. Climbers were stuck in a traffic jam on top of the highest mountain of earth. The traffic jam led to the death of multiple climbers as they were up the peak for too long. Other climbers allegedly had to step over the dead bodies in order to get up or down. While scaling Mount Everest isn't for me, it seems that the once illustrious climb that could only be completed by the world's best climbers has become nothing more than a single list item on a bucket list. Nowadays, the mountain is filled with tourists rather than climbers.

The Mount Everest traffic jam shows us that no destination is safe. Mass tourism is absolutely everywhere and is most problematic where it intervenes with the livelihood of locals. Local residents and their natural surroundings are suffering as a result of our collective urge to travel the world and see its wonders. From the Mona Lisa in Paris to the peak of the Mount Everest, we now have to stand in line to take an Instagram picture— a picture that usually doesn't capture what the experience was really like, that looks exactly the same as that taken by the thousands of other tourists standing next to you.

Overtourism is suffocating the places we love to visit. The old city center of Venice only has about 50,000 inhabitants. Somehow we believe it is OK for up to 30,000 cruise ship passengers to arrive and depart from the city in one single weekend. In Palma de Mallorca, the situation is arguably worse. The small historic town, which has about 400,000 citizens has to deal with up to 1.9 million cruise passengers per year of whom the majority will only visit the famous cathedral in the heart of that old town. Cruises do not start or end in Mallorca, meaning that tourists do not stay overnight, and do not book hotels or spend much money in the local economy. Cruise passengers arrive in the morning and leave in the afternoon, making Palma's tiny streets overcrowded and unmanageable for a few hours each day.

Symptoms of overtourism

Overtourism comes in many forms. It is a relatively new phenomenon that has not received much academic attention about the subject will evolve[17]. This chapter summarizes the research we have come across and combines it with our own experiences to highlight some of its most obnoxious downsides. Over the years, as overtourism is researched more extensively, our knowledge about the subject will evolve.

I have been part of the overtourism problem myself many times, sometimes accidentally, but also on purpose when I wanted to make sure that our data models worked well. Once we had finished the data model for Avoid-Crowds.com, we were able to start predicting which days would be busy and which ones would be extremely busy. The next step was testing whether the model's predictions were accurate. As we finished our prototype in January 2019, we looked at what destinations would be the most crowded according to our models and found a weekend in February—normally low season—that according to our would be extremely crowded in Venice.

Getting to Venice from where we live in the middle of winter is not easy. Living on the northern side of the Alps, and with Venice just on the southern side of the mountains, we ended up driving through a blizzard toward the Italian border. Due to the adverse weather conditions, we were almost the only idiots on the road, and there were no traffic jams nor signs of mass tourism as we conquered the icy Alpine roads. But as soon as we left the mountains behind us and got closer to Venice, we started to notice that traffic was picking up. We arrived early on Friday evening and parked our car at one of the parking garages as you enter the city from the 3.8-kilometer (2.4-mile) long bridge named Ponte della Libertà. As soon as we parked, we could tell that our predictions were correct and that the city was extremely busy.

We found what we were looking for in Venice: major crowds.

On that February day during the Venetian Carnival, it was absolutely packed. It looked like we'd arrived in a movie scene. Everywhere we looked, tourists were dressed up in the most beautiful carnival costumes. Occasionally, the police closed the alleys near St. Mark's Square were closed by the police in order to manage the crowds and we were blocked in by fellow tourists dressed up as large bottles of Bellini, a Venetian cocktail made with Prosecco and peach puree. While the cause of these crowded days in February was obvious—the famous Venetian carnival—we realized that a trip at this time wouldn't be very enjoyable for tourists who weren't aware of the crowds. But we now knew that our data model worked. We had predicted mega crowds and Venice had delivered. Unfortunately, we had to experience it for ourselves and therefore also started to learn quickly about the symptoms of overtourism.

Too crowded

The most obvious symptom of overtourism is major crowds; crowds that are so large that they change the livability of the destination where they occur. Attractions and recreation areas have a limited capacity, which is often not clearly indicated or communicated, and which has limitations. Within those limitations, there are enough facilities for tourists such as hotel beds, restaurants, transportation, and even something as simple as toilets.

Imagine a popular beach. On a normal day, there's plenty of space for everyone, enough lifeguards to keep those in the water safe, and toilet facilities available for all visitors. On a hot summer day, people flock to the beaches and the situation changes. Too many people need to use facilities that have not been designed for major crowds. The lifeguards now have to work overtime and can't guarantee the same level of safety as usual, especially if the warm weather was unexpected. The toilets become unbearably unhygienic and local restaurants will run out of ice cream and cold drinks. What might have been a perfect beach day just a few weeks ago is no longer enjoyable for anyone, and could even be unsafe because the local facilities and authorities are overstretched.

This kind of overtourism can lead to serious disruptions in the area. Authorities may block roads that lead up to beaches to prevent them from becoming overcrowded. Similarly, access to a tourist attraction can also be limited by putting a cap on ticket sales. These kind of caps have been introduced in the years before the coronavirus pandemic, but have been used more and more by governments as lockdowns began to ease. This has serious consequences for tourists who can no longer "just show up" at an attraction, and have to buy tickets well in advance.

Authorities might be able to close streets leading up to beach areas, but they cannot completely seal off a city to all tourists. This kind of crowd control just isn't possible for many of our most beloved tourist destinations, which cannot be closed when the number of visitors reach capacity. This makes the most popular cities like Paris, Venice, or Amsterdam especially vulnerable to overtourism.

The Italian capital, Rome, is a good example of a city that often welcomes more tourists than it is able to handle. Rome is a major cruise destination as Civitavecchia, one of Europe's most popular cruise stops, is located about an hour northwest of the city. Based on our own research, 101 large cruise ships were scheduled to arrive in Civitavecchia in 2020 for a total of over 1,800 times. In total, these 101 cruise ships carry a combined maximum capacity of over 2.5 million cruise passengers. Almost all of these passengers would travel from Civitavecchia to Rome. Although COVID-19 prevented most of these tourists from coming in 2020, under normal circumstances Rome can handle more than 16,000 cruise passengers arrive on a single day. Those 16,000 cruise passengers will all have a similar itinerary that includes only a few of the city's highlights including the Colosseum, Trevi Fountain, Spanish Steps, and the Vatican. Although you might not feel the effect everywhere in Rome, these already busy highlights will become far too crowded when there are lots of cruise ships in Civitavecchia's harbor.

When locations are overcrowded, it's much harder to enjoy the experience. In Rome heavy crowds will usually limit your access to the attraction you travelled all that way to enjoy. At the Trevi Fountain, for example, crowds of tourists will block your view of the fountain. With thousands of tourists jammed into a small square, tourists compete for a spot near the water for their moment to throw in a coin or two for good fortune. To take a picture of the fountain without other people in it, you need to arm wrestle your way forward, to strategically position yourself next to fellow tourists whom you believe may soon leave their prime spot and wait. As soon as you find your spot and take your selfie, you can be sure that other tourists will be patiently, or not so patiently, waiting behind you to take their turn.

Overtourism at the fountain leads to chaos. And in chaotic, crowded situations, pickpockets thrive. Bags, wallets, phones, and cameras are often stolen the moment you have other things on your mind. Tourists are most vulnerable when they are distracted and a beautiful fountain is most definitely one of those places. Meanwhile, the massive crowds give criminals cover to approach their victims undetected and to get away without being seen.

INSIDER TIP: To avoid being pickpocketed, be extra vigilant in crowds. Make it as difficult as possible to steal your belongings. Close your bag and keep your valuables on your person. Preferably in your front pockets, where you have a good view of them. Show potential criminals you are vigilant by looking behind you and showing any suspicious people that you are aware of them.

Real estate prices

Apart from crowds on your holiday, there are other very serious side effects of overtourism that are mostly hidden from tourists. For example when our love for traveling starts to influence real estate prices for those living full time in those places.

Over the last 10 years, a true lodging revolution has taken place. Back in 2010, tourists had a limited choice of accommodation when they visited cities. They had to choose between a hotel, hostel, campsite, or a traditional bed and breakfast. Since then, Airbnb opened up hundreds of thousands of apartments and homes to tourists, pretty much anywhere they'd want to go. Homeowners were introduced to a completely new and highly profitable business model they could take advantage of: short-term rental. While the increased demand for hotel beds increased real estate prices , short-term rentals, like Airbnb, took those prices to a completely new level. In 2019, Harvard Business Review published an article in which three authors explained that when the number of Airbnb listings in a city increase, so do rent prices[18].

Multiple media outlets have covered the negative effects of short-term rental. Although we often refer only to Airbnb, privately owned short-term rentals can also be found on other platforms like Booking.com or Vrbo.com. In 2018, BBC.com[19] published an article describing the negative effects of Airbnb. According to the prominent British news outlet, those critical of Airbnb claim "property owners are switching from long-term tenancies to short-term rentals, which can be more lucrative". This means that landlords are switching from serving inhabitants of the local community to serving tourists instead. As a result, fewer homes are available in high demand areas where prices start to surge as people rent out apartments to profit from the booming tourism industry. The results can be devastating for locals.

With reduced housing supply and rents that are no longer affordable for many, the original inhabitants are forced to move out. The effects are serious and undeniable. The BBC writes that although "Airbnb represents only a tiny percentage of all housing units in any given city, it can represent a very substantial percentage in certain neighborhoods, such as in Barcelona's Old Town". According to a 2015 study cited by BBC.com, 16.8% of all homes in Barcelona's Old Town are listed on Airbnb. The same study claims that short-term vacation rentals have become the battlefront for a new sort of gentrification, where a poorer population is forced out of its neighborhood and replaced by a richer population: tourists.

Short-term vacation rentals also have other negative side effects. While hotels have to adhere to strict hygiene and safety rules, this is not necessarily the case for many renting out their own homes . Furthermore , many Airbnbs are located in apartment blocks, where tourists moving in and out can disturb other tenants and their living environment. Imagine a group of tourists renting an apartment and hosting a party. While the homeowner can take the money and stay somewhere else, their neighbors bear the brunt of the disturbance without any compensation. Guests in hotels and hostels can also cause disturbances, but they usually don't share the building with local residents.

With so many negative side effects, local governments are taking precautions to fight short-term vacation rentals. Cities around the world have introduced legislation to stop or limit the spread of new listings. In most cities, houses and apartments need to get a special license before they may be rented out. In Barcelona, these licenses are no longer provided, limiting the increase of Airbnbs. In Amsterdam, the number of nights where a home owner can rent out their house has been limited to 30 since 2019. Before 2019, that limit was 60 nights.

Despite one of the strictest limits in the world, the battle between the city of Amsterdam and Airbnb has continued well into 2020. Amsterdam newspaper *Het Parool*[20] wrote in early 2020 that Airbnb is not doing enough to enforce the 30 night rule. However, alderman for living conditions in Amsterdam, Laurens Ivens, is quoted saying that "Airbnb is finally recognizing that they are causing disturbances". COVID-19 has changed Amsterdam's approach again. During the lockdown, without tourists, the city of Amsterdam was a completely different metropole. The heart of the city turned into a ghost town as many of the homes that were usually rented out as short-term holiday homes, were left empty. In the aftermath of the lockdown, the municipality of Amsterdam moved forward on a full ban of regular short-term rentals[21]. Only those with a bed and breakfast license are now allowed to rent out their city center homes.

Cost of living and lifestyle

As locals are forced out of city centers, the shops and facilities they previously frequented are forced to adapt, and what you can buy in the center starts to change. A large part of Amsterdam's city center notoriously turned into shopping streets that only cater to tourists and stroopwafel shops are the perfect example. Stroopwafel shops are clearly not targeted at Dutch citizens. As a Dutchman, I can tell you that the Dutch do eat stroopwafels, but we never buy them at special shops. Neither do we dip our waffles in chocolate or decorate them with chocolate sprinkles, tiny marshmallows, or other types of sweets. That is done solely for tourists, who—judging on the number of shops and Instagram photos of decorated stroopwafels—have completely fallen in love with the not so Dutch treat. Dutch people, when they eat stroopwafels, either buy them at the supermarket or at a traditional farmer's market.

And yet, stroopwafel shops have emerged all over Amsterdam's city center. These shops take the place of homes or other shops that no longer have locals to serve. Instead of shops serving the local community, like butchers, greengrocers, or bakeries, Amsterdam now has stroopwafel shops, ticket shops, burger joints, and souvenir shops. This impacts the availability of goods and services the local community needs and makes life harder for those still living in the city center.

The same happens at local supermarkets that do still exist. Normal food gets replaced for groceries that tourists like to buy, such as quick ready meals, bottled drinks, and other more expensive items. Meanwhile, less and less healthy groceries that need proper cooking, such as fruit and vegetables, find their way onto the shelves.

The lack of availability of normal products to the local community has far-reaching effects. The local community not only needs to deal with the large crowds, but living in tourist areas has become more expensive as well. Those staying behind have to pay more rent, their groceries are harder to find, and the price of those groceries has heavily increased .

Environmental

Tourists also produce waste, use polluting means of transportation and—if too many tourists travel into areas with lots of wildlife—kill the animals they come into contact with, even if not purposefully. No matter how you travel, by car, airplane, coach, train, or even bike, your vacation will impact the environment. Imagine you hop on a flight to go on a cruise and take a few excursions on land during your journey across the ocean. Every single step of the way, you will impact the environment.

CO_2 Emissions

Traveling is not good for the environment. Getting to the airport involves taking a car, taxi, bus, or train and flights are notorious for their CO_2 emissions. If you fly in a Boeing 737, the most used airplane in the world, your vacation will cause 115g per passenger per kilometer. At your destination, you might hop into a taxi again and by the time you arrive at your hotel, you have used up trees and fossil fuels and have polluted the air with the CO_2 emissions you created.

Transport Mean	Passengers Average	Emissions (g CO_2/(km·pax))
Train	156	14
Small Car	4	42
Big Car	4	55
Bus	10.7	68
Motor Bike	1.2	72
Small Car (Depending on number of passengers)	1.5	104
Big Car (Depending on number of passengers)	1.5	158
Plane	88	285
Bicycle	1	0

Figure 10: **CO2** *emissions per means of transportation. SOURCE: European Environment Agency 22.*

Cruise ships aren't much better. Although many new cruise ships run on more sustainable liquified natural gas (LNG), most of the operating cruise ships run on much less sustainable diesel and can cause a great deal of damage to the environment. Cruise ships use enormous amounts of fossil fuels. According to Griffith University[23], "an average cruise ship passenger emits 0.82 [metric tons] of carbon dioxide-equivalent for their cruise. This is equivalent to a return air trip from London to Tokyo in economy class." Having said that, Griffith University is also reporting that the two largest cruise ship companies in the world, Carnival Cruises and Royal Caribbean Cruises, "are making improvements in carbon efficiency". Unlike Norwegian Cruise Line Holdings, Carnival and Royal Caribbean publish sustainability reports "that detail annual emissions".

Even when cruise ships are in port, they continue to generate their own electricity by burning fuels in their power generators. Ports too should step up their efforts to supply energy that is produced in a more sustainable way onshore. Unfortunately, there are numerous cases where cruise ships do not use these land lines, even if they are available. One of the reasons is the higher costs associated with using the cheaper diesel generators that the ships have onboard. Where such resources are available, local authorities should enforce the use of these power sources to reduce dangerous emissions in highly populated areas.

Waste

Tourists produce a lot of waste: 35 million metric tons of solid waste globally per year[24]. There are countless reports of waste dumped in nature by tourists or the tourist industry. Within the European Union, tourism accounts for 6.7% of the total waste generated in all member states. While this percentage might seem low, the type of waste they generate is "associated with greater environment impacts", according to the European Commission. Oceans get polluted, beaches and cities get littered with trash, and even the waste that is disposed of in the correct way creates headaches for waste management authorities during peak season. The European Commission adds that plastic waste, generated by tourists in particular, can have an impact on the oceans and "poses a threat to whales, dolphins, sea turtles and birds".

According to the European Commission, waste produced by tourists can cause serious environmental problems. This includes resource depletion, land occupation, soil contamination, water pollution, and air pollution, as well as greenhouse gas emissions. In the last few years, measures have been put in place to reduce the adverse effects of tourism on the environment when it comes to waste. These measures have been successful to some extent, but there is still a long way to go.

In its report *Linking tourism and sustainable waste management,* the European Commission published[25] an overview of best practices for hotels to reduce the amount of waste they generate. This includes some simple, straightforward and smart ways of working. As tourists, we can help hotels with many of these points while challenging behavior that has a negative effect. Packaging alone accounts for up to 40% of a hotel's waste stream according to the travel foundation cited in the report.

Department	Measure	Description
Housekeeping	Efficient bathroom toiletries	Replace individually wrapped soaps and shampoo dispensers. Provide additional toiletry items only on request
	Efficient housekeeping	Avoid use of bags in bins, or where used, replace only when solid
Catering	Provision of low impact drinking water	Avoid bottled water as much as possible. Provide guests with tap water in rooms and dining area (may be filtered and bottled) and provide reusable glasses for drinking
	Efficient breakfast provision	Avoid single-person servings as far as possible within hygiene constraints, and cook to order. Avoid single-use plates, cutlery, etc.
Reception	Efficient document management	Print documents only when absolutely necessary, double-sided in small font. Use electronic billing
Procurement	Efficient ordering and storage	Order perishable products only in quantities required. Store perishable products in appropriate conditions. Order non-perishable products in bulk
	Local sourcing and packaging return	Source food locally where appropriate and return packaging for reuse
	Select low packaging products	Select products with less packaging where possible and consistent with other green procurement criteria, e.g. purchase chemicals in concentrate form

Figure 11: How hotels can reduce waste. SOURCE: European Commission report.

Figure 11 gives a good overview of where hotels can make an effort and how you can have an impact. Reducing and properly disposing of waste is one of the easiest ways to reduce the impact we have on the environment as we travel. Avoid single-use plastic and challenge your hotel, airline, or cruise company when you witness behavior or procedures that harm the environment.

Think about all the untouched food that is thrown out from buffet breakfasts or food and drinks which rot away because of failed procurement. Unfortunately, the recent pandemic has cancelled out many of the advancements made in the last years.

Environmental friendly travel is now under pressure. We might travel less during a pandemic, leading to reduced CO_2 emissions, but single-use plastics are on the rise again. The pandemic is "threatening hard-fought victories that restricted or eliminated single-use disposable items", Smithsonian Magazine wrote in May 2020[26]. Plastic bags have returned to supermarkets, and Starbucks has paused the use of reusable cups[27] "as cities in the US have temporarily suspended almost 50 single-use item reduction policies".

I am under the impression that hotel breakfast buffets that were becoming more and more sustainable before the pandemic, now turned into plastic buffets. At a well-known hotel in Copenhagen, Denmark, single-use plastic gloves needed to be worn to serve your own breakfast. In Italy, we had to use single-use plastic cutlery. Meanwhile, there are many single-use products that work just as well as plastics. This includes using recycled plastic, wooden cutlery and other solutions that are less destructive to our planet. Sustainable single-use protective gear prevents the spread of the virus just as much as the more widespread, non-sustainable plastic knives, gloves, plates, and forks.

In popular destinations, the waste from hundreds of thousands of tourists can accumulate very quickly and local authorities may struggle to deal with it. As tourists we can remind hotels and others in the tourism industry of their duty to care about our planet.

Infrastructure problems

Imagine that five cruise ships arrive in a harbor at the same time. These five ships need supplies and all the guests need transportation for their excursions. Five cruise ships with 3,000 cruise passengers each means 15,000 cruise passengers. You need about 300 buses to transport all of those passengers to local attractions and the result is a major melt down of traffic in and around the cruise port. Roads will be blocked and residents will struggle to get around their city. Unless the infrastructure is upgraded to deal with these large influxes of tourists, cities will suffer.

It's not only the cruise industry that is causing infrastructure problems. For years, Italian cities have suffered from too many tourists driving into and parking in historic city centers. This has lead not only to traffic jams but also to residents not being able to park in front of, or even close to, their own homes. Authorities around the world have been experimenting with different solutions to mitigate this effect.

While my mother was able to drive into Pisa's city center in 1965, that is no longer possible. In Italy, tourists are no longer allowed to drive into the centers of cities like Florence or Pisa. They are now designated zones where only those living in the area are allowed to drive. These zones are known as "Zona a Traffico Limitato" (ZTL). Driving into one of these areas without the right permit can result in heavy fines, as my sister discovered when she went to Pisa 55 years after my mother. Without paying too much attention to the ZTL zones, she drove into the heart of Pisa with her husband and three kids. As the streets got narrower and the area got more difficult to navigate or drive, she realized she'd made a mistake. The situation got worse when my sister got stuck in a tiny street. When asking locals where to go, the only answer was "not here". Only when they started asking for "autostrada", which translates to "highway", was my sister shown the way out of the tiny alleys and onto the streets leading out of Pisa. Unfortunately, while navigating Pisa's tiny streets, the car had passed a ZTL check point and about 12 months later, on her birthday, she received a gift from the city of Pisa: a fine of about 100 EUR for illegally entering the ZTL.

INSIDER TIP: Some parking garages within the ZTL areas in Italy are accessible without the right permit. The garage registers your car with local authorities as you park. We successfully parked next to the famous Duomo cathedral in Florence using this system.

In Amsterdam, another kind of traffic is blocked from entering the city center: coaches. Coaches carrying large groups of tourists became an increasing problem in the Dutch capital. Six percent of all tourists in Amsterdam use coaches[28]. With limited space, these coaches are competing with other kinds of traffic, causing big problems in the city's small streets. According to Amsterdam city council, this leads to deteriorated quality of life in the city. As a result, all coaches will be banned from the city center from 2025 onward[29].

My mother, uncle, and grandparents visiting Pisa in 1965.

Most cities in Europe are not equipped to handle mass tourism. As the cities grew organically in the middle ages, mass tourism was not on the minds of city planners. Narrow streets, cobblestones, and alleys are not made to sustain the flows of large crowds. Local residents trying to live their everyday lives are often blocked by walking tour groups, touring buses parking or stopping in the middle of the road, and traffic jams as a result of too many visitors. As a resident of Salzburg, I was once late to work because there were two Sound of Music hop-on hop-off buses blocking the road.

Avoid being part of the overtourism problem

Overtourism is not just caused by an increased number of tourists, as urbanization and increased tourism go hand in hand. In fact, the majority of residents in the cities most affected by overtourism believe there shouldn't be limitations to the increase of visitors[30]. In stead we should focus on better managing tourism rather then limiting it. Local governments are trying to find ways to mitigate the effects or, in some scenarios, simply turn a blind eye to the problem. But World Tourism Organization (UNWTO) Secretary General Zurab Pololikashvili says "tourism can only be sustainable if developed and managed considering both visitors and local communities."

This means that we, as visitors, can make the cities that we visit a little more sustainable. We can be responsible tourists. There are simple things that we can do to help, and these are likely to enhance our own experience. A true win-win situation. So, what is it that we can do? How can we have a positive effect instead of a negative one?

What we can do
How we can minimize our own impact when it comes to overtourism

Clean up
Dispose of your trash the right way. Don't litter

Think about others
Don't be loud in residential areas. People live there

Culture
You are the visitor. Try to understand the local community so you can respect it

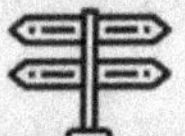

Alternative destinations
Travel where others aren't going

Think about where you sleep
Short-term rentals might negatively effect local communities

Help each other
Sometimes we're not aware of what we're doing and need some help. Don't assume people know

Travel outside Peak Season
Travel when most others aren't there

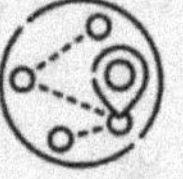

Don't block streets
Don't block streets with your car or tour group

Although we can't stop the rise of tourism, as tourists we can do things to reduce the impact we have on our destinations. There are some very easy rules to follow when traveling to minimize your impact:

Research local laws and customs

As tourists, we know that we don't do everything right. Cultural differences, different laws, and unknown history can make it difficult for tourists to understand how they should behave when visiting a new country. In Asia, for example, the rules for visiting a holy site can be confusing: sometimes you are not supposed to wear shoes and sometimes shoes are mandatory. On our honeymoon in Sri Lanka, my wife and I learned that you are not supposed to take a photo with your back to Buddha but it is OK to face Buddha sideways. We also learned that, according to local customs, you should not use Buddha statues to decorate houses or gardens, which is something that you frequently see in Europe. All in all, cultural differences can be confusing, but they're also part of what makes traveling so exciting.

When you travel from the United States to Europe or vice versa, the cultural differences are generally not so big, but they can still be complicated. In some countries you are allowed to drink in the streets, but in others you can get arrested for doing that. Having a picnic or sitting down to eat a sandwich in public areas is also not allowed in some cities and countries. In your home country, it might be totally normal to show affection in public but it may be frowned upon at your vacation destination. Sometimes you can freely fly a drone to take photos, but in other areas you might go to jail for it. It is just not possible to know how we are expected to behave without some consideration in advance and doing some research.

While Venice is doing a great job telling tourists how they should behave, most cities just assume that you know how. This can cause a lot of confusion, misunderstandings, and heated discussions with locals telling you off in a language you don't understand. I have been yelled at in plenty of local languages many times for breaking rules I still don't know anything about. It isn't easy.

First and foremost, tourists need to be respectful to the destinations we visit. You should behave in the way you would want tourists to behave if they were in front of your house. You can also do some research on local customs and local laws in advance. The easiest thing to do is to buy a travel guide. Travel guides, like those published by Lonely Planet, often give you do's and don'ts. You can also go online and Google what to do and what not to do.

Local governments can't always be relied upon to inform visitors how they are supposed to behave, and you are likely to find that you are shouted at or fined regardless of whether you were aware of a rule or not. It is also worth checking the travel recommendation of your own government. The FCO in the UK and the State Department in the US have detailed pages on local laws and customs that can help tourists. They also include essential information on possible risks and precautions that you might need to take.

Don't litter

This is the easiest and most important thing you can do: keep the place you are visiting clean. Don't litter. If you have trash, use a bin. It's not normal to litter back home, and it isn't normal on vacation either.

Don't disturb others

Playing loud music, shouting to your friends in the street late at night, or other anti-social behavior isn't going to go down well with locals, whether you're at home or on vacation. If you would be unhappy with someone doing it outside/next door to your home, then don't do it outside/next door to someone else's.

Don't block the streets

If you're part of an excursion or traveling with a group, make sure you're not physically interrupting daily life in the city. Make way for locals on their daily routine.

Go off the beaten path

One of the main strategies used by cities to mitigate the effects of overtourism, is to promote the dispersal of visitors within a city and beyond. This is a promising approach as research has shown that tourists are happy to oblige and may even be willing to pay more to avoid crowds[31]. So how do cities do this? They often host events away from the city center, develop alternative attractions, and introduce city-wide or regional travel cards for tourists.

If we are honest, we often visit a city to see the main sights. Going to Paris without visiting the Louvre or the Eiffel Tower is not a realistic option for most travelers. But combining your visit to the Eiffel Tower with visits to lesser-known attractions is a good idea.

Around the main tourist sites, you will not encounter locals or have an authentic experience of what it is like to live in that city. But seeing a bit more of what the city has to offer, will give you a fuller experience and will lessen the impact on the areas around the main tourist attractions.

Choose a hotel over a private short-term rental

Short-term rental companies like Airbnb have caused major disruptions in the travel industry. The once mighty hotel industry now has a competitor that has changed how we travel. Some of that change is good. More competition means lower prices, which enables more people to afford a vacation than ever before. In addition, houses that would otherwise be empty are now being used.

Unfortunately, there is a flip side as well. Short-term rental has not only disrupted the travel industry, but also societies. For many homeowners in city centers or near tourist hotspots, it has become economically attractive to rent out their apartments on a short-term basis. Investors have even started to buy up accommodation near hotspots specifically for this purpose. As a result, real estate prices in those areas started to rise and the local population can often no longer afford the rent in the area they have always lived in. In addition, mass tourism has taken its toll on the livability of areas with lots of short-term rental units.

Now, renting accommodation on a short-term rental website is not necessarily bad. But you should think carefully before booking. Are you renting the home of someone who just happens not to be there for that time period? Maybe that person is on a business trip, or there is another plausible reason for that home being rented out. As long as the owners of the apartment stick to local regulations and are not just out for a quick buck, Airbnbs can be a great alternative. But it becomes a different story when you are renting an apartment that is clearly only there to serve a single purpose: making profit from tourists. If you are looking at a place like that, you should think about the impact it is having on the local community. In those cases, hotels are better. Hotels are regulated and new hotels often have to comply with lengthy procedures before they can open their doors.

Use your camera the right way

In the future, we are likely to see cities promote alternative hotspots more and more. As tourists we can help them draw other tourists away from the most popular spots by visiting these alternative sites and promoting them by posting about them on our social media accounts. Think about it: if we post realistic photos on social media, they will probably show our friends overcrowded pictures from the main attractions and nicer photos from the alternative sites we visited.

Think about where you sleep

An easy win for us tourists is to think about where we sleep. We can easily book our accommodation away from the crowds. In Barcelona, you don't have to stay on Las Ramblas. Try a hotel just outside the city center with easy access to public transport. You will save money and minimize your impact on the livability of the city at the same time. A win-win again.

Don't travel in peak season

Another strategy used by local governments is to try and spread out the tourist visits throughout the year, as well as geographically. In general, they promote experiences during off-peak months and try to actively discourage people from coming when it's already busy.

Promoting the off season is the most positive way for them to do this. Cities can host major events like festivals or marathons when only few tourists are in town or offer deals that they hope will encourage tourists to change their plans for summer and try alternatives like spring or autumn instead.

A more negative way to force tourists to change their schedules is to actively limit access to main attractions in peak season or to close off parts of the city. In 2018, Venice took the infamous decision to install turn stiles to limit the number of visitors[32]. This is a more intrusive, but certainly very effective, way to deal with overtourism. Cities are also introducing time slots for popular attractions. It's a less radical approach, but it can still negatively affect tourists' plans to see their favorite sights.

Obviously, not traveling in peak season is not always an option. Unfortunately, many parents are limited to school vacations and are unable to visit tourist hotspots outside peak season. But other travelers do have a choice and if you do, you can and should rethink your travel schedule. By avoiding peak season, we are already minimizing our impact on overtourism.

Help each other

If you see other visitors struggling or unknowingly breaking rules, you can help them before they get in trouble. In a friendly way, you can tell them how the locals might perceive their behavior and what they could do to change that. In Venice, for example, you aren't allowed to eat on steps in the streets. If you see someone doing that, you can help them by pointing them to a place where they can eat and keep everybody happy.

AVOIDING CROWDS WHILE TRAVELING

Sometimes, it's impossible to avoid crowds. Many people don't have a choice about where or when to travel if they have business or family reasons, or are limited to going on vacation when their children are in school. That means traveling in peak season, when most destinations are overly crowded. But even in those situations, there are ways to escape the crowds. You just have to plan a little, do a bit of research, and be willing to be flexible.

Avoid crowds while traveling

Plan ahead
Before you go, think about what you're going to do

Start early
Mornings are best to travel without crowds, even on the most crowded days

Doing less = more
Spend more time at your destination and experience more

Alternative destinations
Travel where others aren't going

Small tour groups
Get more attention and easily navigate the city without causing a disturbance

Sleep away from the crowds
The prices are lower and you benefit from not waking up among mass tourism

Stay longer
A longer stay creates more opportunities for authentic experiences

Plan ahead

Planning your vacation ahead of time is more necessary now than ever. Even before the pandemic, many tourist attractions started selling timed entry tickets and some even limited the number of tickets available for any given day. Without some research and planning, you could find yourself spending hours waiting in line to buy a ticket. Even worse, you might not even be able to see the attractions you want to see at all.

I found this out myself on a three-day trip to Machu Picchu while I was in Peru in November 2019. Unlike before, you can't visit Machu Picchu without very detailed planning. Due to overtourism concerns and to protect the site, Peruvian authorities started limiting the number of tourists that could visit the famous 15th century citadel per day. One of the measures was to stop selling tickets at the entrance. Tickets need to be bought online or in the town of Cusco, three and a half hours by train away from the ancient ruins.

Aguas Calientes, a small tourist-focused town at the foot of the mountain that is home to Machu Picchu, would be perfect for selling tickets to Machu Picchu, but you can't buy them there at all. Apart from food and shelter, the only things sold in Aguas Calientes are souvenirs and tickets for the bus that takes you from the town up the mountain to the entrance of Machu Picchu.

Peruvian authorities are trying to preserve the UNESCO World Heritage Site by capping the number of tickets sold per day. Those tickets are then also spread over the day and limited per hour. On my journey to Machu Picchu, I also wanted to climb the famous mountain peak you see behind the citadel on most photos. This mountain peak, called Huayna Picchu, is only accessible by a dangerous winding path full of big steps and small climbs. To ensure the safety of hikers and to preserve the site, tickets for the mountain are limited to only 200 per day, divided over two slots. Because these tickets are limited and get sold out, you have to buy a ticket well in advance or risk not being able to access the site on any of the days you're in the area.

In Peru, planning ahead is essential. Without preparation you risk not being able to see what many see as the highlight of Peru. This is the case for many other destinations too—planning ahead will save you time and effort, and will allow you to make most of your stay. Find out where you will need tickets and buy those before you even leave your home. Vacation time is too valuable to waste on waiting.

Major crowds in Prague in the summer of 2019.

Start your day early

Perhaps the easiest way to avoid crowds, even during the busiest months, is getting up early. Most tourists simply don't do mornings. They are either enjoying breakfast, busy checking out of their hotels, or haven't even arrived in the city yet. Cruise ships usually arrive in port in the early morning, but these ships are not immediately cleared by local authorities. That means cruise passengers and cruise excursions won't be hitting the city streets until a little later. There are also fewer tourists in the morning than in the afternoon. That is because departing tourists are busy preparing to leave on the morning of their departure and not doing any sightseeing. Meanwhile, arriving tourists will not be able to check into their hotels until 3 p.m. or later.

Starting your day early might not be the first thing you think of when you're on vacation and being able to get up late at least once is probably the number one thing you're looking forward to. Nevertheless, mornings are golden! Waking up early allows you to beat the crowds and experience a city without mass tourism while at the same time enjoying golden hour; the hour after sunrise has beautiful natural light where the angle of the sun makes the world looks golden. Empty streets and golden sunlight will help you create the best Instagram shots you've ever taken.

I love walking through cities in the morning. The one city where I love those morning walks the most is New York. My favorite days in New York start when I walk out of my hotel into Manhattan's streets as early as possible. Before all the shops are open and before most people have even arrived for work, I get to walk around and see how the city wakes up. My favorite moments are when the doors of metros and trains open and locals step out to get a coffee on their way to the offices and shops they work in. New York City is at its most photogenic as the first rays of the sun burst into the island's streets. While it must be an evil part of my soul that loves seeing others go to work when I'm enjoying a vacation, it's the closest that I will get to truly experiencing life in the city.

Manhattan might not be the first place you think about when we talk about overtourism, but New York attracts over 67 million tourists per year[33] which is slightly more than the international visitors in the whole of Italy each year[34]. Most of them only get to experience Manhattan and will only see Queens or Brooklyn from the inside of a cab as they travel from JFK to their Midtown hotel. Those arriving at Newark will likely see no other borough than Manhattan, other than on their inevitable visit to the viewing platform at the top of the Rockefeller Center.

INSIDER TIP: Make the most of morning golden hour. Waking up early has multiple advantages, but for those traveling with their camera, early mornings give you the best light to take breathtaking pictures.

Quality over quantity: less is more

You can do more during your vacation by choosing to do less. It sounds like a contradiction. How can you possibly see more tourist attractions in a limited time if you decide to do less? Imagine being in Paris for only two days. You decide to make a list that contains the most well-known tourist attractions in the French capital. The list includes the Eiffel Tower, Notre Dame, Versailles, Montmartre, the Moulin Rouge, the Catacombs, Sacré-Cœur, and most definitely the Mona Lisa at the Louvre. If you want to fit in all the attractions on your itinerary, two days will be tight, but you might actually make it to see all eight. The problem is that if you do, you still will not have experienced Paris.

The price you pay to make it to all eight attractions is that you don't have the time to truly enjoy the attractions you came to see and experience. You have to slow down to make sure you have enough time to see the beautiful gardens around Versailles, or the time to get lost in the streets of Montmartre, or to see the Eiffel Tower from the other side of the Seine River.

The Mona Lisa is the perfect example. The painting is most definitely an extraordinary piece of art, but it shouldn't be on any list of things to see in Paris. Instead of the Mona Lisa, the Louvre Museum should be on your list. The Louvre itself is world famous and worth spending time exploring. The famous Da Vinci portrait is surrounded by some of the world's best paintings, but many tourists won't even see those pictures. The situation has become so bad that the New York Times posted an editorial in which it argues that it's time to remove the Mona Lisa from the Louvre.

With as much as 80% of visitors to the Louvre only interested in Mona Lisa, NYT's Jason Farago argues that the painting is not located in the right place. According to Farago, "the Louvre is being held hostage by the Kim Kardashian of 16th-century Italian portraiture: the handsome but only moderately interesting Lisa Gherardini." Farago argues that the Mona Lisa should be placed in her own building, fit for the massive modern-day crowds. The building can have timed entry, moving walkways, and corporate sponsorship. That would allow the Louvre to breathe again, while giving the masses what they want: just to see the Mona Lisa.

Unless you go just to see a single piece of art, a proper museum visit takes time. Planning more time to see what else a museum has to offer in addition to the world famous pieces of art might open your eyes to artists and artwork you didn't already know about—art that might inspire you, upset you, or that shows you the world from another perspective. Staying longer in the Louvre will add to your backpack of knowledge and experiences that makes your next trip to another museum even better. The

Louvre will allow you to relate to experiences and understand history better, but only if you do it right.

Near the Mona Lisa you also have one of the largest paintings you will ever see: the Coronation of Napoleon. It was that picture that I remember most about the Louvre. As a child, I was taught at school that Napoleon crowned himself as emperor after which he crowned his wife Joséphine as empress. Like many pieces of art in the Louvre, it is a history lesson written in paint. The Louvre has hundreds, if not thousands, of these history lessons in its collection. Rushing in and out of the museum to see the Mona Lisa is an insult to history.

The problem is that long list of attractions you have to see—paintings, landmarks, and landscapes that you have already seen on tens of thousands of images, but need to see with your own eyes. Slowing down means that you can't make some of these pictures, some of those selfies and that you can't show your Instagram or TikTok followers that you crossed that landmark off your ever-extending bucket list.

Of course, there's nothing wrong with selfies or lists. My only plea is to not try to cross everything of your list as fast as you can. When you slow down, you're able to look around you while you travel. When you're in Paris, see what Parisians do. Observe their behavior and try out what they do as you visit their capital. This allows you to get another view of Paris, something a bit more authentic. When you see how other communities eat, drink, and speak, you open up your heart and mind. For the days that you're there you can be part of the community and bring home those experiences rather than just selfies.

Also never forget that, if you're traveling to a destination, the road leading to that destination might be worth a destination too. When you don't take your time, you won't be able to view and interact with that environment. A trip like that is less valuable. Stop halfway on your trip between attraction A and attraction B. Step out of the metro, car, or bus and experience what life really is like at your vacation destination. Of course, make sure it's safe to do so first. Always do your research about where it is safe to travel and where it is not, and stick to guidance by your government and local authorities.

Try alternative hotspots

If you want to experience real life in Europe, leave the city centers and skip some of the most crowded destinations. Divert from the beaten path and explore new parts of a city, region, or country. That way you will not only beat the crowds, but you will also have a unique experience.

At some picture-perfect tourist destinations, you may not be as welcome as you might think. In early 2019, media outlets around the world were reporting that the mayor of Hallstatt, Austria, was asking tourists to stay away[35]. According to these media outlets, the picturesque lake village had been completely overrun by tourists. The village has a population of just 780 and attracted a mere 100 tourists per day back in 2008. The village is now a UNESCO World Heritage Site, featured in some very popular TV shows and the alleged inspiration for the major Disney movie Frozen. As a result, Hallstatt now attracts over 10,000 visitors a day; a number the small village cannot cope with, mayor Alexander Scheutz reasons.

The mayor intends to put measures in place to keep tourists from coming to Hallstatt. Entry for coaches filled with tourists has already been limited by the introduction of a system with time slots and reservations. Meanwhile, the mayor is also considering road closures as he explains that the village is not a museum but "an important piece of cultural history." Scheutz also realizes his options for deterring tourists are limited: "We want to reduce numbers by at least a third but we have no way of actually stopping them", he told the Daily Mail[36].

In 2006, Hallstatt featured in a popular South Korean TV-program, inspiring a Chinese company to build a complete replica of the village in 2011 at a cost of almost 900 million US dollars. This attention has made Hallstatt an incredibly popular destination for travelers from Asia, with tourists coming from China, Hong Kong, Japan, and South Korea. But it was after it allegedly inspired the magical city Arendelle in Frozen that visitor numbers really exploded, and images of the village went viral on Instagram. According to the Daily Mail, the village has been dubbed the "most instagrammable" place in the world and now attracts six times more tourists per capita than Venice, while hotel rooms cost between USD 320 and USD 450 per night.

Hallstatt is situated in the Salzkammergut region near Salzburg in Austria. The village is overrun by day-trippers that usually take a bus tour from Salzburg, Vienna, or elsewhere. The tiny town has put a drone ban in place and has posted rules and behavior guidelines at the entrance of the town. You can also find local shops catering solely to the influx of tourists. For example, there is a shop where you can rent a dirndl or lederhosen (traditional Austrian clothing) for just an hour. All these tourists shops market toward the mostly Asian audience.

So, why not skip Hallstatt and go to any of the surrounding lakes instead? The water in the lakes in the Salzkammergut region is of extremely high quality and all of them are surrounded by beautiful mountains. At Lake Wolfgang, a 33-minute drive from Hallstatt, the water heats up to a comfortable 23.9 degrees Celsius (75 Fahrenheit) in summer. Unlike the lake at Hallstatt, you are allowed to undertake endless types of water sports activities on Lake Wolfgang, including renting a boat or trying to balance on a stand-up paddle board.

At every major tourist destination in Europe, there are alternatives either within cities or nearby. Barcelona has a beautiful coastal line; north and south of the city are coastal towns surrounded by nature. Venice is surrounded by beaches where Italians love to spend their summer, and destinations like Florence or Pisa are situated in the middle of Tuscany, where the countryside, dotted with medieval structures, is a destination by itself.

Even within cities, there are areas that are worth visiting away from the crowded historic city centers. That is the case for almost any city in Europe as well as in the US. Most people tend to just visit one area. Most New Yorkers would argue that to truly experience the city you have to explore one of the boroughs outside of Manhattan. Of course, in any large city there are some areas that are better to avoid for safety reasons, but this shouldn't hold you back from wandering into other, les frequently visited, parts of town. You can easily find out online what else is worth a trip or find your information through an old-fashioned travel guide. It's only outside the tourist areas that you can truly experience what life at your destination is like.

Choose small tour groups

In the age of overtourism, we should be mindful of the impact of our presence on local liveability at a destination and the experience of other tourists. A common complaint from locals is large groups of people navigating through small streets, blocking them up, and making life harder for those actually living in the places where we vacation. This has become such a big issue that the city of Amsterdam has even banned tour groups from the Red Light District—to be clear, overtourism wasn't the only reason why the city of Amsterdam banned group tours from the Red Light District (the main issue was respect, or lack thereof, for sex workers).

The city has also introduced stricter rules for tour groups in general[37]. The rules, introduced in 2020, mandate a maximum tour group size of 15 participants, as well as a special tour group tax that essentially eliminates the practice of free tours. The tax is said to be EUR 1.50 for each participant. In addition, tour guides need to be registered at the Dutch chamber of commerce. The city is also exploring the potential introduction of a mandatory quality mark. These measures, while effective in the areas they target, seem to have moved the problem to other parts of the city and authorities now aim to deal with the problem once and for all. Similar measures were taken for the Statue of Liberty in New York City. Speaking to CNN[38], a representative of the Statue of Liberty Park said: "Commercial guided tours add to the congestion in these identified areas and prevent the free flow of visitor movement and impact public programs and the visitor experience".

As tourists, we have the responsibility to make sure we minimize our impact on daily life at our destinations. Moving in large groups, blocking roads, and stopping local inhabitants from going about their daily business is not the way to go. A free group tour might cost you nothing, but the city will pay the price.

Not only are smaller groups the better option for the city, they're also often of much higher quality and better for us as tourists. Large groups will follow a pre-arranged route. Day in, day out, the tour guide will visit the same highlights and will tell the same stories over and over again.

When touring in smaller groups, you'll find that your tour is more personal. You'll have the opportunity to ask your guide all the questions that come to mind and they will have the time to answer them. Smaller groups have a more intimate atmosphere that often results in the sharing of personal experiences, insider tips, and other information that might go beyond the scope of regular tours. You will certainly hear anecdotes from your guide and the other tourists in your group that might inspire you to explore other sights and activities in the city. Tour guides leading small groups are generally more willing to share their secret spots, like the best local restaurants and the prettiest shops and boutiques to get your one-of-a-kind souvenir.

It's not always easy to find small tour groups. You will have to do a bit of research. If the tour isn't advertised as a "small group tour" or with a maximum number of participants, there is a high chance you will end up in a big tour. Tours by bus or coach are never small. Coaches easily seat 50 people.

So how to find small group tours? Sometimes it's easy: the title of the tour might include "small group" or even "private tour". Otherwise, you can find clues in the description of the tour, or you can contact the tour organizer and ask. If that doesn't help, check the reviews. I would also encourage you to review tours. When you review a tour, you can leave hints behind that make it easier for other travelers to see if it is what they are looking for. Always try to be honest about whether a group was too big, blocked roads, or caused other annoyances.

Don't use free tour groups

The phenomenon of free city tours has been popping up all over the world. A free tour means that you show up at a set time at a set location, the tour starts, and you decide what you want to pay at the end. What you want to pay might be nothing, in which case the tour is free, but most people decide to pay so that the tour guide makes money. Unfortunately, it's not as simple as that. Behind many of these tours, there is a shady scheme.

Usually these tours are organized by companies that want to profit from mass tourism and they often spend lots of money on marketing. They produce high quality flyers, make billboards, and actively use online ads to target tourists. So how is this all possible? How can they spend so much money on marketing if the tours are free? Well, actually free tours are highly profitable. Let me explain why.

To understand how money is made from free tours, you need to understand the business model of these companies. Businesses offering free tours usually hire low-cost tour guides—foreign students, for example. These students then get a crash course in becoming a tourist guide and after getting a bit of experience, when the company deems them good enough, they can start giving tours. These tour guides, hired by the "free tour company" pay for the possibility to do these tours. For each guest they show around, they need to pay a fee to the company. This means that your tour guide invests in the group he is showing around. Let's say that they need to pay 3 EUR per person per tour. A group of 20 means your tour guide owes the organization 60 EUR before they make a single cent for themselves.

This means that the tour guide has great incentive to give you a really good tour. The tour guide is already down 60 EUR, and they know that they need to earn at least that much to get their money back. At the end of the tour, the tour guide will ask the group to pay whatever they like, but in reality they need to earn an average of at least 3 EUR per person to break even and may try to make you feel guilty for using their services for free. If you pay very little or insist that your tour was for free and do not pay, they make a loss on your participation. This explains why tour guides will often put pressure on you to pay.

You might wonder how the business that organizes the free tours knows how many people are in the tour group. This is usually assessed based on the semi-mandatory tour group photo taken at the beginning of the tour. With that photo, the organization can count the number of participants and charge the tour guide accordingly. Other ways of checking group sizes including registration and using publicly available webcams to count and track the movement of tour groups.

It is essential for these free tour companies that they get enough people to sign up for the tours. The bigger the tour group, the bigger the return on their investment. Unfortunately, the bigger the tour group, the less enjoyable it is for the tourists. Another trick that free tours and low-cost tours use to make money is taking their groups to tourist traps, where the company will earn a commission over your purchases.

Free tours don't offer value for (no) money. These tours are only sustainable because they are cheap to organize, attract big groups, take advantage of you and the guide, and make money by visiting tourists traps.

As a result, these tours follow a very similar path with the same stories and the same sights every tour.

The quality is also often poor. In many cities, guides don't need any form of certification, which means that anyone can become a tour guide. But even if tour guides are certified, why would a highly qualified professional give tours for free? They make some money, because you are pressured into tipping at the end, but how much they get depends on the group, and more tourists mean more money. If someone is a pro, they wouldn't think twice about charging for their expertise, right?

There are exceptions. Sometimes municipalities offer free tours to encourage tourism in their cities. For example, cities that are not your typical bucket list destinations will pay tour guides in order to make the city more attractive. In other destinations, volunteers will share their passion for their beloved cities. Most of these initiatives are not heavily marketed and can't be found in Europe's biggest destinations.

INSIDER TIP: Don't be tempted to go on a "free" tour. It is never really free. Your guide relies on tips, and you are asked to pay "whatever you can afford" at the end. Consider whether a highly educated, skilled, and trained tour guide would offer her or his services for free. There are of course exceptions but generally speaking free is never really free.

Sleep away from the crowds

Tourist crowds usually don't spread evenly throughout the city. If they did, we wouldn't have so many problems. You can usually find the tourist crowds around the main highlights or tourist attractions that a city has to offer. In Barcelona, that's around Las Ramblas and the Gothic Quarter, in Amsterdam, it's the area around central station, and in New York, it's the area around Times Square. Tourists cause sound disturbances, block pedestrian areas, and most locals will try to avoid the area because of the many tourists there. These extremely crowded areas can be found in every single tourist destination, usually at the heart of a city, at the main boardwalk, or near a famous tourist attraction. What you can also find in these areas are hotels.

Unless you absolutely require a hotel with a view of all the tourist chaos, I would recommend booking your hotel elsewhere. Of course, you won't be able to book a room with a view—at least, not one of a landmark like the Eiffel Tower, Times Square, or the Rialto Bridge. But those rooms can only be booked at the centrally located hotels at a massive premium anyway.

Sleeping away from the action helps you avoid crowds. If you pick your hotel a few blocks, or even just a road away from the main attractions, you won't be staying in the middle of mass tourism. Instead, you're usually in an area that's quieter, more authentic, and much more affordable. The further you get away from the action, the cheaper your hotel.

Of course, picking a hotel too far away from the city is also not a good option. While these hotels might be more economically priced, you can spend that saving again on your transportation costs but with proper infrastructure, like a good metro line, it's no problem to be further away from the center. Do your homework before you book. Check what public transportation is available that can take you to and from your hotel. Don't just check if there is a line available, also check how long it will take and how much it costs. If you have to pay 40 dollars on transport to and from your hotel, it is worth staying closer to the action if the price difference is less than 40 dollars. If the bus that takes you to and from your hotel doesn't operate on weekends, that hotel is not a good choice for a weekend trip.

Sometimes staying in the city center is worth it for reasons other than cost. In Venice for example, tourists can opt to stay in Mestre. Mestre is located just outside Venice on the mainland and therefore, if you stay in Mestre, you are kind of missing the point. Mestre is not Venice. Staying overnight in Venice allows you to go to bed and wake up in the city. It should be part of the experience! In big cities like Berlin or New York, that is much less the case.

It's best to find a balance: a hotel that's near enough to the attractions you want to visit, but far enough away from the pricey chaos of overtourism. I would recommend doing your homework before you book. Is your hotel located near public transport that will allow you to go in and out of the city in no time? How do the transport costs weigh up against the money you will be saving on the hotel? How will staying outside the city centeraffect your overall travel experience? After answering those questions, you can make a properly informed decision.

Get to grips with hotel room prices

It's not always easy to understand hotel prices. Hotels use dynamic pricing, meaning that rates go up automatically when demand is high and drop when demand is low. In addition, hotels will try to differentiate the prices of rooms within the hotel, with different categories that can be sold at a premium. Some rooms are obviously going to be more expensive—think about a suite versus a standard room. But other rooms are exactly the same apart from the view out the window.

INSIDER TIP: Hotels are very creative in coming up with fancy names for their worst rooms. Be on your guard when you book rooms that have a view in their description: garden view, patio view, courtyard view, urban view. You either pay a premium for the best view, or you are about to book no view at all.

For consumers, it is almost impossible to understand all the different elements that influence hotel prices as not all of these elements are publicly known. It is, for example, impossible to know as a guest when events like conferences, weddings, or business meetings are scheduled at a certain hotel. Supply, demand, and competition heavily influence hotel prices and hotels have access to extensive databases to finetune their pricing. Having said this, there are many building blocks of hotel pricing that we are able to understand. So let's explore some of them:

Seasonality

Seasonality is one of the easiest building blocks of hotel pricing to understand. Hotel prices go up when it's busy and go down when there are fewer tourists to lure in. Supply and demand in the tourism industry relies heavily on seasonality as public holidays, school vacations, and local events bring more tourists to hotels, causing increasing prices. Prices drop to their lowest point during low season.

Location

As set out earlier in this chapter, location is also an important building block. Real estate prices around tourist hotspots are higher, but the foot traffic makes them attractive places for investors to build hotels. To make a return on these pricey investments, investors need to ensure that the hotel generates enough income. This is something that is reflected either in smaller hotel rooms (and therefore more rooms to sell per square foot) and/or higher room rates.

Hotel branding and star rating

Another building block of hotel prices is the star rating. When you book a room in a hotel with a one-star rating, that hotel will have minimal amenities, fewer services, and probably less luxury and comfort. At the other end of the spectrum are five-star hotels. These luxury hotels charge more but also have more facilities, more luxurious rooms, and extra services like spas, swimming pools, and gyms. In addition, you pay a premium for hotels with a good reputation and brands that have been carefully built over the years.

Room type

Room types are another building block of hotel price. Rooms that are bigger, and have more windows or a better view, are usually priced higher than others.

It is not always easy to navigate the different options when booking, so it's worth checking the detailed description of each room. An executive room might be one square foot bigger than a standard room, but sold at a serious premium. Check what you get for each price point and contact the hotel if you have questions about the rates.

When you arrive at a hotel and your room is not what you expected, it's because there's a mismatch between your expectations and how the room was communicated or marketed to you. While the hotel might try to blame you for not understanding the offering, it is not your responsibility to properly communicate what the product is that you buy. In these scenarios, complaining in a polite and calm way almost always helps. Explain what you expected and the mismatch you experienced with what was delivered.

INSIDER TIP: Don't settle for a room that you didn't choose. Always make sure the hotel knows about your dissatisfaction and be clear that it is their problem, not yours. Always remain polite and calm.

Booking type

Another way to differentiate pricing and maximize profit for hotels is to play with different booking types and associated rates. Pre-paid hotel rooms give hotels the guarantee that the room you booked is paid for, no matter whether you show up or not. They transfer the risk of a no-show to you, which is usually compensated with a lower hotel price. Rooms with more flexibility are usually more expensive, as the hotel runs the risk of losing money if it is cancelled.

Breakfast and other extras

Booking with or without breakfast is another factor. When breakfast is included, the hotel usually charges more, but you get an extra product (breakfast) in return. You determine the value of the breakfast. What are you willing to pay for breakfast, and is that worth the difference in hotel rates? Sometimes other services are also included in the room rate. This can include dinner, museum packages, spa treatments, or even all-inclusive drinking packages. Some of these packages are worth it, others are not. It's up to you to determine whether the package represents value for money for you or not.

Special rooms

Some hotels market rooms as extra special, for example because it has a desirable view or a celebrity has stayed in it. The premiums for this type of room can be insanely high. It's up to you to determine whether that premium is worth it. Many of these rooms are special suites or bungalows. In the Maldives, most hotels are marketed with beautiful pictures of bungalows right over the sea. Those are very often special bungalows away from the main building. While rooms in the main building are affordable, those bungalows over the ocean are sold at a premium that many cannot afford.

Stay longer

It might sound strange, but even the most crowded destinations become more enjoyable when you don't have to rush. Why? When you stay longer, you slow down. You don't need to run from landmark to landmark. Your stay will be truly enjoyable, rather than a bucket list challenge. When you allow yourself an extra day or two, you have the time to adjust to your new environment and the chance to relax and enjoy your trip.

When we try to pack too much into short vacations, a lot of time is spent waiting in line or buying tickets to access all the sights you want to see. When you stay longer, you can slow down and buy tickets when there's no line or visit the landmarks when they're quieter. When you stay longer, it's not just the highlights that you can visit. You can really become part of a destination. When in Rome, you can see what the Italians do throughout the day. You won't see that if you're rushing from the Vatican to the Colosseum.

AVOIDING TOURIST TRAPS

Christopher Reynolds from *The LA Times*[39] once wrote "Overtourism, like pornography, may be difficult to define, but you'll know it when you encounter it." I believe the same can be said about tourist traps.

Tourist traps are those overpriced attractions, restaurants, and bars that are solely there to persuade tourists to enjoy a not-very-genuine experience. Tourist traps sell pricey goods and services that are purely targeted at tourists. Unfortunately, they come in many forms. It can be a restaurant, a souvenir shop, a bar, or an actual attraction. The things all these tourist traps have in common is that they are strategically located and that their prices are usually much higher than the local average.

Tourist traps are best avoided. Not only will you spend more than necessary on your vacation, they're generally just a waste of your valuable time. When you decide to go to the torture chamber in the Amsterdam Dungeon, you support their business, which pushes other traditional business out and occupies valuable local real estate.

Once you're able to recognize tourist traps, you can avoid them and go for the genuine experience.

How to recognize tourist traps

Tourist traps are both expensive and crowded. The good news is that most tourist traps are easy to recognize. The number one question to ask is: are the tourists there because of the attraction you're looking at? Or is the attraction, shop, or restaurant there because of all the tourists? That is the sole question that needs to be answered.

When you visit the historic city centers of Amsterdam, London, or Prague you will see the same type of tourist experience in every city. Wax museums and torture museums or dungeons are everywhere, which means the experience they give you is not an authentically local one. Often, these experiences are even offered by the same companies in different cities. The Amsterdam Dungeon can be found in York, London, Hamburg, Edinburgh, Blackpool, San Francisco, Berlin, and even Shanghai. The Dungeon is merely there because of the tourists.

There are also lots of tourist trap shops. These small shops offer overpriced products to tourists and tourists alone. They are usually late-night convenience stores that are operated in city centers. They offer a mix of groceries, (mainly alcoholic) beverages, and souvenirs. Local residents do not frequent these shops. They know their way to the regular supermarket and are aware of the price differences.

Another infamous tourist trap is the restaurant that offers menus in multiple languages. Menus that are translated from the local language to English or a single other common language are not unusual, but when there is a version in Spanish, French, German, Arabic, Chinese, Greek, Romanian, Turkish, Russian and Japanese, you're probably about to walk into a tourist trap. Another giveaway is a restaurant that has translated its menu in picture form. These types of restaurant are infamous for selling low quality food at high prices. It's better to skip these restaurants and opt for something more local. Use a translation tool like Google Translate to overcome any language difficulties if needs be. Not only will you pay less, but your experience is going to be more genuine.

Another way to recognize a tourist trap is to look at the clientele. If a bar or restaurant attracts lots of locals, it probably isn't a tourist trap. If there are only fellow travelers, it's probably not an authentic local business.

It is unlikely that you'll be able to avoid all tourist traps as you travel. The tourism industry has grown so rapidly and has taken over entire areas of cities. Local genuine businesses are pushed out and overpriced restaurants, tuk-tuk rides, and torture museums have taken their place. Smart entrepreneurs have bought property around the most frequented areas in the world's most popular tourist destinations. Their goal is simple: to take advantage of the booming tourism industry.

Nothing about these attractions is authentic or historic. Without tourists, these attractions would disappear. Genuine businesses, that do not only cater to tourists, would survive even without international visitors.

INSIDER TIP: Common sense is your best weapon against tourist traps. Ask yourself: are the tourists here because of the attraction or is this attraction here because of the tourists?

DOING YOUR RESEARCH

With 1.4 billion international tourist arrivals across the world every year[40], it's safe to say that traveling is not something you do alone. Unless you actively seek out alternative destinations, you will meet fellow tourists, with whom you will be competing for the best seats in restaurants, the last empty stools at the bar, swimming pool beds, and your moment to get an unobstructed view of the Mona Lisa.

So how do you make sure that you will win that competition? How do you beat the crowds? The answer is: by doing research. The more you know about the destination or landmark you're visiting, the more you're able to get the most favorable view, deal, seat, or table. Sometimes that might mean paying a premium price, but most of the time it simply means making an online reservation or showing up early. We don't recommend waking up at 7 a.m. when the pool opens to join the towel battle so you can claim valuable pool real estate, we mean being an informed tourist that knows what he or she is doing. When traveling, knowledge is power!

Your crowd-beating tool kit

Most of your research should start before you even book. What do you want to visit? What do you want to do? Once you know that, you should pick accommodation that allows you to do what you've planned. The length of your stay should also reflect your plans. Consider which days you'll be staying and what that means for your vacation. Weekends aren't great when for shopping or to visit museums. Meanwhile, cruise ship crowds make some afternoons extremely crowded.

You've booked your vacation, you know where you're going to be staying and how long you'll be there. Now it is time to make some firmer plans. Here are some of the tools that we use to avoid crowds while on vacation.

Crowd-beating toolkit

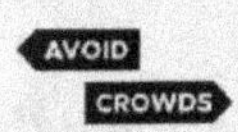

Avoid-Crowds.com

Check how busy your destination gets each day. Like a weather forecast, Avoid-Crowds.com predicts mass tourism. This includes cruise ship arrivals, public holidays, events, and school vacations

Travel blogs and websites

There is an almost unlimited amount of blogs available to help you

Cruise websites

Check which ships will dock during your stay so that you can avoid too many cruise passengers

Google Maps

Navigate through the streets of your destination but also see whether attractions are busy or not

Ticket sites

Avoid spending time in lines, by buying your tickets in advance

Attraction apps

Theme parks and other attractions offer apps that show waiting times, tips, and much more

Avoid-Crowds.com

The number one tool I am going to shamelessly plug in this book is our own. Avoid-Crowds.com is the best tool for avoiding crowds because our website gathers all the information for you in one place. You can see which days are expected to be crowded and which days are better.

To give you these crowd predictions, we combine lots of different data sets from the tourism industry. We collect data on school vacations and public holidays, which we combine with historic hotel occupancy rates and publicly available data on tourism flows. We enrich that data with information on local events and cruise ship arrivals. And like a weather report, we predict when there are going to be crowds and when it's going to be quieter.

At Avoid-Crowds.com, you simply select a day and a destination and we'll give you a crowds score from 1 to 100. 1 means very quiet, while 100 means extremely busy. Not only do we give you this simplified score, but we also explain why it's going to be busy, for example, because it's a national holiday or because there is a marathon in town. With that information, you can plan smarter. A marathon won't influence how busy the local museum is, but a national holiday will.

Travel blogs and websites

Travel blogs and travel websites offer a rich resource for things to do and experiences for any given destination. Why not read or watch the experiences and lessons of others before diving in yourself? You can learn a lot by reading about other people's lucky finds or biggest mistakes.

You can find blogs, videos, and news articles about your destination by using Google or searching on YouTube. Search for things to do, attractions to visit, and museums that you should not skip. Travel blogs and websites can also offer tips on areas to pick for your hotel as well as restaurants and local dishes to try.

To ensure you don't just get the most mainstream ideas for your vacation, we recommend digging a bit deeper. This is easier than it might sound and just means asking Google a few other questions. Search terms that will help you find alternatives to the main highlights are:

"What alternative attractions can I visit in [DESTINATION]?"

By "alternative attractions", we mean those attractions that are beyond the most visited highlights. These lesser-known tourist attractions are usually less crowded and give you a more authentic local experience.

"Where locals go in [DESTINATION]"

Why not learn from residents of the destination you're going to visit? Search on Google for information about what they do. There will be plenty of local bloggers that want to show off parts of the city that are less well-known to most other tourists.

"How to avoid crowds in [DESTINATION]"

Overtourism and crowds are topics for many bloggers and news outlets nowadays. You'll find plenty of tailor-made tips and tricks that apply to the destination you are visiting.

"What to do when you visit [DESTINATION] for a week?"

A week is a long time for any city trip or single destination vacation. When you search for a longer period than one or two days, you will start to find alternatives to the most frequently visited hotspots that most tourists will go toduring their one or two days there.

You have to be careful when you do your online research. Many influencers and bloggers are invited to destinations by third parties, such as train lines and hotels, for the purposes of advertising to tourists. The views of these bloggers therefore might not be as unbiased as you think, especially as blogs and news sites do not always properly disclose sponsored articles. Even highly respected traditional media sometimes fall into this trap.

On the evening of July 18 2020, Amsterdam was so crowded that Amsterdam authorities had to take extreme measures to stop massive crowds from coming to an already full city, according to an article published on local news channel AT5.nl[41]. This, however, did not stop *The Guardian* from telling a completely different story. On that same day, the respected British newspaper[42] published an article about Amsterdam as a "crowd-free joy". Amsterdam is not free of crowds and the measures the city had to take now hugely impact a visit to the Dutch capital. Alleyways leading to the Red Light District are closed[43], street artists can no longer perform[44], and the major shopping street, Kalverstraat, and the streets in the Red Light District are now one-way only[45]. Furthermore, the city has invested heavily in COVID-19 hosts, who guide domestic and international tourists in an attempt at crowd control.

If *The Guardian* had done some fact-checking, they would have come across the countless social posts and articles reporting massive crowds in the city. Locals complain relentlessly about the return of (mass) tourism on Twitter[46]. Local city councilor, Don Ceder, came across these articles and went to see for himself. He posted that, although the city had taken lots of measures and the COVID-19 hosts are now on the streets, it was impossible to keep a safe distance from others early in the evening, even though crowds are usually lower then than late at night. A video he added to his tweet shows the overcrowded streets. Later that evening, the city of Amsterdam urged people not to come to the area at all anymore because it was too crowded.

So why did The Guardian tell such a different story? The newspaper took the offer of a free Eurostar ticket and free hotel room at Conscious Hotels Westerpark and sent one of its reporters to the city that she argues is seemingly empty. It's likely that both the hotel chain and the train company wanted to boost their occupancy as they're suffering from lower bookings due to COVID-19. The news article that followed, reads more like an advertorial than the high standard of journalism we are used to from *The Guardian*.

It describes some parts of Amsterdam that are quieter than before the crisis hit, like the Rijksmuseum and Tropen Museum, and also says that the local markets are attracting fewer tourists than before. Reactions to the reporter's article on social media already show that, thanks to her publication, at least one tourist is now considering going to Amsterdam as the city is "a crowd-free joy".

The problem is not so much what *The Guardian* wrote. You can indeed enjoy parts of the city without crowds. The problem is that *The Guardian* is only highlighting the angle desired by the hotel and train company that paid for the visit, while ignoring the emerging problems caused by the increasing amounts of tourists in the city. Overtourism has already returned to Amsterdam despite the pandemic, and the situation is so intense that the municipality has been forced to fight back hard with disruptive measures to protect its citizens. This superficial article in a major UK publication will lead people to believe that Amsterdam is empty, when the opposite is true.

You can imagine what travel bloggers and influencers are willing to write in exchange for a freebee if even *The Guardian* can be persuaded by a free train ticket and free night in a hotel. Always be cautious about blindly trusting what you read and see. Check whether a post is sponsored, a hotel night is paid for, or if the blogger receives any other form of compensation. Although this type of cooperation between the tourism industry and journalists, bloggers, and influencers is completely fine, it needs to be disclosed so that readers and viewers can make up their own minds.

The Guardian did disclose the information, but seemed to have forgotten that they are also journalists who should look at the situation from more than one angle. A month after the article, new outbreaks of COVID-19 were holding a tight grip on the Dutch capital again. The situation got so bad that on August 18, the mayor of Amsterdam announced additional measures and asks tourists to stay away[47].

Cruise websites

For destinations that we have not yet added to Avoid-Crowds.com and that often have cruise ships traveling in and out of the local harbor, there are other sources to help you identify when it will be busy. Cruise websites show when what ship is in which port. You can find many of these websites by searching for your destination in combination with the words "cruise schedule".

Once you know when what ship is where, there is one additional step: you also need to research the size of these ships. Ships with a large capacity, measured by the number of passengers, bring more tourists into town than others.

It's worth knowing that cruise passengers will not stay all day. Most ships arrive in the morning and leave in the afternoon. This means that passengers need to get back to their ships well before departure time. As a result, it will likely be very busy from late morning till early afternoon (10 a.m. until 3 p.m.), but by late afternoon and during the evening, the cruise passengers will be back on their ships.

On busy cruise ship days, we recommend exploring the less popular attractions in town. Keep the highlights and main attractions for the days that you're not competing with cruise excursions and thousands of other cruise passengers exploring the cities by themselves. It's also a good idea to skip the area around the port just after arrival of the cruise ship and before its departure.

INSIDER TIP: When cruise ships are in town, most passengers will limit their day trip to the most popular tourist destinations and skip the less popular areas in town. These are the perfect days for you to visit the less well-known attractions.

Google Maps

Google Maps serves two main purposes. The tool helps you get familiar with the layout of a city beforehand, and helps you to navigate between your hotel and the sights you want to see. You can use Google Maps, or any other maps tool, to get familiar with your surroundings. But Google Maps also allows you to make complete routes that take in all your plans for the day. You can plan a route that takes you from attraction A to attraction B to attraction C and more. You can load your bucket list into the app and plan the quickest route that ensures you'll see your entire bucket list.

Google Maps call this feature "Directions". On its website, Google writes that "You can get directions for driving, public transit, walking, or biking on Google Maps. Whenever you see multiple routes, the best route to your destination is blue"[48]. You can make the route using directions on the Google Maps website and then send it to your phone or tablet to view on the move. Together with the GPS on your phone, these routes can make your navigating the streets at your destination much easier while ensuring that you won't accidentally skip a landmark you want to see.

Google Maps has another useful feature. The app and website show you which hours of the day are usually busy at the tourist attraction you intend to visit and which times it is usually quieter. The crowd feature uses real time data to tell you when it is less busy or more crowded than expected.

Pre-buy tickets and excursions at GetYourGuide, Viator, and others

There are lots of websites where you can buy tickets and excursions before you even leave home. By buying tickets before you leave, you can save valuable time researching your options while you're trying to enjoy your destination. Websites like GetYourGuide and Viator sell tickets from local companies offering their services and different excursions through their websites.

Simply fill in your destination and the dates you'll be there, and you'll get endless options of excursions, tours, and tickets. You'll also see star ratings from previous users, which allow you to compare the quality of the services on offer. Be aware that the price might be higher or lower when you change the number of participants. A private tour with one person is considerably more expensive (per person) than a private tour where you are able to fill a van with five people, for example. With five people, you share the total price of the private tour with four of your friends or family rather than paying the full price yourself if it's a one-person tour.

INSIDER Tip: Compare the price of your tour on different websites. You might be pleasantly (or unpleasantly) surprised by pricing variations.

Apps and websites of attractions

Most museums, landmarks, and tourist attractions have websites. Some even have their own apps. These websites and apps usually give you all the information you need to plan a visit, including opening hours and security information, and you can often buy tickets directly from the attraction you want to visit. At the moment, these websites and apps are also the best place to find the most recent information on temporary closures or pandemic-related rules that are in place.

Although a lot of tourist attractions have really good websites, I have noticed that many others do not. During the COVID-19 pandemic, we created an overview of which tourist attractions were open and closed that included about 110 European landmarks. Many websites offer pop-up messages saying that the attraction was closed or only open with limited capacity. And, in addition to the very basic information about closures, lots of websites also offer extra information pages explaining the rules that are put in place to fight the spread of the virus such as mandatory face masks or social distancing.

Unfortunately, there are also a lot of websites that don't give you correct information. Some attractions have outdated websites that don't provide anything meaningful at all, while others offer up-to-date information in the local language, but fail to provide that information in English or other common languages among international tourists. In those cases, it's easiest to either contact the attractions directly or to do some additional online research.

While some attractions aren't able to provide proper information, theme parks usually have superb information available to their visitors. Through free apps on Android and iOS, users can often get a digital map of the theme park including information on all the rides, services, and available food and beverage stands. This information includes who can or cannot go on a certain ride as well as opening hours and information on how long visitors have to wait in lines. The wait times are updated real time so you can adjust your plans accordingly. Some apps even go as far as predicting how busy it will be in the coming hours so you are even better informed.

INSIDER TIP: Going to a theme park? Download their app a few days before you go. See how long the wait times are for the rides you want to go on and adjust your plans according to that information.

Buying tickets

To avoid crowds while on vacation, one of the best things you can do is avoid waiting in line. Your vacation time is too valuable to waste. Standing in line to get access to an attraction is one thing, and might even be difficult to avoid. But there is one line that you can easily avoid in 2020, and that's the line to buy an entry ticket. Almost every attraction in the world now sells tickets online and its rapidly becoming standard. It might even be your only option in the future.

With overtourism problems looming, tourist attractions need to find the balance between making a profit and preserving the integrity of the experience or attraction they sell tickets for. One of the strategies they can adopt is limiting the number of tickets they sell. With limited tickets sold, authorities can manage tourism flows better and protect our beloved monuments.

With COVID-19 now also a worry, more attractions need to limit the number of tourists that can visit, particularly enclosed spaces. Museums like the Rijksmuseum in the Netherlands, for example, have been forced by the government to only sell a limited amount of tickets so they can enforce social distancing and stop the virus from spreading.

I would highly recommend buying tickets to the attractions you want to visit in advance. You risk not being allowed in otherwise. This is, for example, the case at Machu Picchu where tickets are not even sold at the entrance of the archaeological site.

As ticket sales have moved online, new services have been introduced to generate additional income for the attractions. But there are so many different types of tickets that you can buy and it can sometimes be confusing to navigate the websites that sell them. There are standard tickets, timed entry tickets, and even "skip the line" tickets. Some tickets come with extras such as a free drink or full flexibility. How do you know which ones are best for you?

Standard tickets

Standard tickets are the simplest, old-fashioned entry tickets. There is nothing special about standard tickets. You buy a ticket that allows you to enter a certain site. These tickets usually don't have a time or even a date associated with them. You book the ticket online, print it out, and bring it to the entrance of the attraction. Based on the capacity of the attraction, you are either let in immediately or you have to wait in line until there is enough room to let you in.

Standard tickets are disappearing as lots of ticket offices at major attractions move online. This means that you can often no longer buy tickets at the door of the attraction that you want to visit. Instead, tickets are sold through the official website, as well as through official and unofficial resellers. It is best to buy tickets through official channels. Vending machines for buying tickets are also popping up at many attractions, but have more recently been taken out of service due to COVID-19.

Timed entry

Timed entry tickets are a solution to one of the biggest annoyances I have while on vacation: waiting in line. My wife and I learned the benefits of timed entry tickets at the Vatican in 2016. Before we hopped on a cruise across the Mediterranean, we spend a few nights in Rome. It was not the first time I'd visited Rome, but it was the first time I could enjoy it properly. I'd previously visited Rome with my father, but had broken my shoulder blade in a road cycling accident just days before our flight. Even worse, the hospital had made the wrong diagnosis, and I was in agony as I waited for the pain in my body to magically disappear like the hospital had said it would. In Rome, my father was able to show me most of the highlights, but standing in line for a long period of time was not something I was able to do. And the biggest line I had ever seen in my life was the line in front of the Vatican Museum.

The line at the Vatican Museum, which is also home to the Sistine Chapel, starts inside the museum building, where you are forced to zigzag through a maze of other visitors for hours. But before you are allowed to enter the Vatican Museum's maze of queuing tourists, you need to wait outside first. And the line outside the Vatican Museum is endlessly longer. You can't see the end of the line from the beginning, nor the beginning of the line from the end.

The queue outside the Vatican Museum crisscrosses in front of the building and then continues down the street. As the queue nears the end of the road, it takes a turn around the corner, where it follows the massive medieval outer wall of the Vatican until the next corner. As the line rounds yet another corner, tourists get trapped between the massive Vatican wall and the bustling traffic of Rome. The line only usually comes to an end after yet another corner.

Standing in that line is not easy. Especially if you've broken your shoulder blade. When my father and I witnessed the long queue and decided to call it a day, we didn't have a smartphone in our pocket. When I found the same queue again in 2016, things had changed. As tourists stood in line, dozens of street sellers were asking whether they were interested in "skipping the line" as though they somehow had a magic trick to get you out of waiting. As experienced travelers, my wife and I are always on the lookout for scams and so, while standing in the long line in front of the

Vatican Museum, we did some research online. On the website of the Vatican Museum, we were able to buy tickets for certain time slots and somehow (perhaps divine intervention?) a slot was available within an hour. We left the line and enjoyed a coffee and a sandwich in a nearby café as we waited for our moment. At exactly the time we'd booked, we skipped the line by passing right by it. The street sellers smiled at us as they recognized that we understood their trick: they asked for premium prices for time slot tickets that were available to anybody online.

Just a few years ago, not many tourist attractions sold tickets based on time slots. In 2021, time slot tickets will be the standard for most attractions. We bought timed entry tickets for the Shard in London and lots of other attractions around the world. COVID-19 will almost certainly result in more attractions adopting advance and timed entry tickets in order to avoid people lining up in close proximity to each other, where a virus can easily spread. The risk of transmission between tourists can easily be reduced by eliminating those lines. I would not be surprised if no tickets are sold at the Vatican Museum's doors anymore in the future.

INSIDER TIP: Even if you are already standing in line. It is always worth checking whether there are still tickets for timed entry on your phone. You might be able to skip the line at no extra costs.

Tips for timed entry

- Plan your visit early; availability will reduce as the date gets closer.

- Buy from the attraction's website or authorized resellers. Other sellers will charge an avoidable premium price.

- Mornings are quieter.

- Read the details carefully. Sometimes you need to show up earlier than your pre-booked slot.

- If you are planning to visit multiple attractions in one day, be mindful of how much time you want to spend at each one. An observatory platform takes much less time than a museum.

- Allow time to travel to and enter the attraction. Consider how crowded it might be and leave additional time for security, cloakrooms, etc.

- Don't make the mistake of buying tickets with the same time slot for two different attractions!

Skip the line

Opinions about skip the line tickets are mixed. These tickets wouldn't be necessary if there was no line to begin with and these tickets are a way to monetize an inconvenience caused by the attraction itself: waiting. When you think about it like that, skip the line tickets are either a smart way to squeeze an extra buck out of tourists, or the concept is morally dubious at best. The sale of skip the line tickets to those who can afford them is most certainly not an incentive for management to get rid of the line for the rest of us.

Regardless of what your opinion is on these kind of tickets, the important question to answer here is whether skip the line tickets are worth it. Skip the line tickets come in many forms. They can be called premium tickets, fast-track tickets, royal tickets, priority tickets, or perhaps something even more creative. In the end, they all offer the same service. The tickets allows you to avoid the regular line. Sometimes this includes a red carpet you're allowed to walk over ahead of regular tourists, but in other circumstances, the majority of tickets sold are premium tickets and you end up standing in a premium line rather than bypassing anyone.

The annoying answer to whether the extra expensive skip the line tickets are worth it is that it depends on the line. I've seen plenty of fancy priority entrances with red velvet carpets and illuminated signs that remained completely empty while the normal line was unmanageably long. In all those cases, I would happily buy a skip the line ticket and pay premium so that I didn't have to wait. In the case of the Vatican Museum, I would be willing to pay double if I didn't have stand in the searing Roman sun for three hours. But there have also been cases where I've arrived at a tourist attraction afterpaying 20% more to skip the line and found nobody in the regular line at all. I once spent lots of extra money to buy a premium ticket for Universal Studios and had this happen. I've never felt so disappointed arriving at an attraction.

I'm sure there hasn't been much research on how common it is to pay extra to skip the line only to find out that there isn't one to skip, but it must happen a lot. It has certainly happened to me on multiple occasions. Sometimes there's a line, but it's so short that you end up joining it to access the attraction with the people who just turned up, because otherwise you'd just be standing in your special premium line next to them for a few minutes. At that point, you're not only annoyed about having wasted money, you also want to hide the fact that you're one of those idiots that overpaid to skip a non-existent line.

So the most important step to take before booking this type of ticket is to make sure that there is an actual line to skip. That means doing some research again. At the Vatican Museum, younger me with the broken shoulder blade did that research the painful way—by actually going to the entrance of the Vatican Museum and observing the line before deciding it was really there. Nowadays, Tripadvisor and other such travel forums are your friend. Google the attractions, read some blogs, ask on social media. Research is easier than ever before! The time of day too might affect the length of the line. During less popular times, usually in the early morning, it's generally not worth buying a skip the line ticket because you won't have to wait as long.

Even if your research shows that it's likely that there will be a line and it's worth paying more to skip it, be prepared for the possibility that you show up and there isn't one. There's no guarantee. Look at the positive. Even if there's no regular line to skip, it still means you'll get in quickly and it will be less crowded. Just make sure you're happy with the amount you'll pay before you pay it with this in mind, and never pay more than you can really afford to end up getting the same service as everyone else.

Skipping the line by buying a guided tour

Another trick, or hack, to skip the line is by doing something you probably wanted to do anyway: buy a guided tour. Tour guides are often allowed to fast-track lines. At Pompeii in Italy, I witnessed tour guides aggressively plowing through the masses of people in front of the entrance gate, followed by several apologetic and awkward-looking tourists who were now de facto skipping the line. When those tour guides tried to push past me, I purposefully blocked their way, as I was under the impression that they had no right to do so but the guards and ticket officials at the attraction certainly didn't seem to care what was happening in the line.

I'm still not sure whether the ancient city of Pompeii officially offers faster access to those that hire a tour guide, but other attractions definitely do—for example, the Sagrada Família in Barcelona. Quicker access for tourists with a guide is common practice, but you should always double check whether it's official at your destination. Otherwise you might end up blocked by an annoying Dutchman like me who thinks his interpretation of the rules is better than the professional delivering the tour that's the highlight of your vacation.

VIP entry

Many tourist attractions also offer other types of special tickets. For a premium price, you can buy tickets that come with extras. Not only do you get skip the line access to the attraction, but you might also get to stay longer or have a free drink.

We have never been happier with a VIP-style ticket than when we visited New York City's One World Observatory the night after seeing the ball drop. On January 1, after a long night in Times Square, we thought it would be a good idea to go up to the top of One World Trade Center in downtown Manhattan. As we fought our New Year's hangover, we went downtown with our "All-Inclusive Experience" tickets printed out.

All-Inclusive Experience tickets at One World Observatory are sold at a premium. While a regular ticket is sold for USD 38, the VIP ticket costs 58 USD. The all-inclusive VIP ticket guarantees priority lane access for security, elevator, and also exit. The ticket also includes a 15 USD credit to be spent on food, drinks, or on merchandise in the gift shop. Most importantly, it gives you the freedom to arrive at any time on the selected day, which was great for us as it took a little longer to shake off the previous night's overindulgence than expected.

January 1 is a busy day in New York City. When we arrived at the entrance of the observation deck, there was a long line of fellow tourists standing outside in the cold. But with our premium tickets, we were up the tower in no time. Even though we were still suffering from the alcoholic drinks the night before, we were able to enjoy it. It would most definitely not have been so enjoyable if we'd had to stand in line for hours. VIP-style entry on that day was an absolute blessing.

But there are some things to consider before buying VIP entry or skip the line entry. You are buying a ticket to bypass a line. While you might be able to afford these tickets, many cannot. Be aware of that privilege you are able to buy when you walk ahead of a long line of fellow travelers who are not so lucky.

TRAVELING DURING AND AFTER A PANDEMIC

As I write this chapter, it is not yet clear exactly how COVID-19 will impact tourism in the longer term. The situation is in a constant state of flux. When I started writing this chapter, we could still travel freely throughout the European Union as most of the lockdowns and travel restrictions had been lifted. By the time I was finishing the chapter, travel restrictions had returned and being able to produce negative coronavirus tests or undergo mandatory quarantine was the new normal. The only certainty during the pandemic seems to be that the virus is constantly changing where we can travel to, how we can travel, and what we can do once we've arrived.

Within Europe, lockdowns started to ease from June through to early August and tourism started to pick up again. Unfortunately, a second wave now seems to be hitting the continent in August and September. Although it's unlikely that borders will close again to the same extent, travel will remain challenging for the foreseeable future. As I write this section, American citizens are banned from entering into the EU. Although travel has picked up a little, the overtourism problems of the past years temporarily ceased to exist and will probably not bounce back immediately after the crisis is over. It will take some time for the tourism industry to fully recover. In the immediate aftermath of the pandemic in particular, crowds will be smaller as the international appetite for travel has taken a major hit.

In the summer of 2020, my wife and I were able to do some traveling. While closely following the COVID-19 rules, we traveled in and out of five countries, including Italy where the pandemic hit early and hard. Wearing a face mask, I boarded six flights and checked into about eight hotels. Our experience has been very mixed. Hotels, airlines, and other tourist hotspots do their utmost to keep their guests happy and deal with ever-changing industry rules. This results in a balancing act, which not everyone in the tourism industry copes with very well.

I have no medical background and the available information changes constantly. In this chapter you read about our experiences. When you travel, always stay up-to-date about rules and regulations at your destination as well as in your home country. Closely follow those regulations and do more rather than less. Any information in this chapter might be outdated or proven wrong after publication as the global society continuously improves its knowledge about the ongoing situation.

When we started traveling again in late May, hotels in many countries were still shut or had only just reopened to tourists. We noticed quite some changes as the tourism industry learned to deal with the pandemic and all of its consequences. While many believe we should not be traveling at all during the pandemic, expats like us don't really have a choice. Not traveling means not seeing our friends and family for extended periods of time. For us, traveling is a way of life, and within Europe it was possible to travel for touristic reasons at any time. I understand that's something that some might frown upon, but we did it and enjoyed it. As soon as we were able to, we started traveling again while always closely following all rules and regulations. We wore a face mask, practiced social distancing, and kept our hands clean at all times. One thing that's clear is that the rules are different in each country and continuously change. In Austria, face masks are mandatory on public transport as well as in supermarkets. In the beginning, you were required to wear a face mask as you entered a restaurant or bar, but that rule was quickly abandoned in Austria whereas it never changed in Germany. You can now easily recognize a German guest in an Austrian restaurant; they will be the ones wearing a face mask as soon as they leave their table.

It's not just the rules about face masks that change all the time. With authorities starting to understand more about the coronavirus and how it spreads, the rules are adapted. Both in the United States and Europe, rules can be different from state to state, province to province, and city to city. It's not easy to know what rules apply where and when without doing some serious research in advance.

In this chapter, we summarize the most important things we've experienced and have added some useful information, tips, and tricks to make traveling as safe and convenient as possible during and immediately after the COVID-19 pandemic.

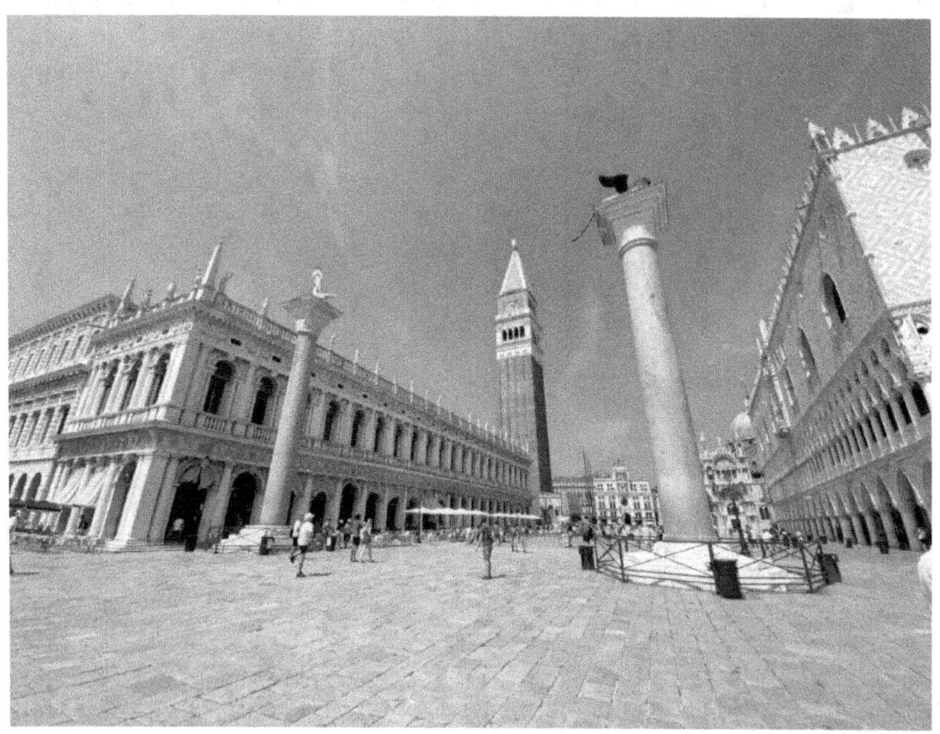

No crowds in Venice after the lockdown in the summer of 2020. Photo by: Marianne Schrama

Avoiding crowds

Avoiding crowds has become a hot topic during the pandemic. Governments and health experts are actively advising us not to mingle. Large groups of tourists are now a problem for all involved. Meanwhile, authorities are trying to get the tourism economy back on track. Maintaining safe numbers of visitors and keeping money coming into areas that rely heavily on tourism can sometimes conflict. Traveling through Europe when the lockdowns eased, we learned a few things about crowds.

It can still be busy, sometimes even extremely busy. There have been reports from popular tourist destinations that at times the crowds grew too large and social distancing was impossible. That was the case in Amsterdam, for example, where authorities were forced to seal off certain areas of the city to deter visitors. Similar stories came out of the island of Mallorca where tourists joined major parties, Portugal—where beach parties allegedly caused a second wave of the coronavirus in the country, and the United Kingdom, where thousands of day-trippers flocked to the beaches on hotter days.

It is noticeably particularly busy at locations that attract lots of domestic tourists, like beaches and resort towns as they're popular among people from nearby cities and villages. In northern and western Europe, shopping malls and city centers have become extremely crowded once again as well.

In southern Europe, in countries like Italy, the contrast could not be greater. Pisa, normally one of the most crowded cities in Italy, was deserted when we visited in early July. The city has multiple parking areas for coaches and tourists coming in from outside the city before they walk into the historic town to see the Leaning Tower.

During the summer of 2020, these parking lots were empty. There wasn't a single coach that brought in tourists from outside Europe. The little white trains that take tourists from the parking area to the Leaning Tower are gathering dust in the middle of the parking lot. At the tower itself, there is almost nobody there. Even in peak season, even during the weekends, the archaeological site and surrounding streets remain empty.

The situation in other Italian cities is no different. Before the coronavirus pandemic, the city of Florence attracted about 16 million visitors per year[49]. When we were there in the summer, we were basically alone. Walking on Ponte Vecchio in 2020 is a unique experience in that you do it almost by yourself. That would have been unthinkable in the previous years as the number of tourists rose ever higher.

But when we look at the usual travelers to Florence, it's no surprise that the numbers have dropped so significantly. The biggest group of tourists that normally arrives in Florence are Americans, who were banned from entering Europe during the pandemic. The same goes for the large number of Chinese tourists who regularly visit the city. Florence also usually welcomes a large number of cruise tourists from the ports of Livorno and La Spezia.

All in all, 2020 is a unique year for tourism. Almost all cities are now reporting much lower numbers of tourists. For the first time in a long time, a city trip to Venice, Florence, or Pisa is a very pleasant experience again that is not negatively affected by large numbers of fellow tourists. Overtourism problems have temporarily disappeared.

Whether tourism bounces back after the pandemic depends on both the length of the coronavirus crisis as well as the travel appetite of tourists. Despite some obvious concerns, there are signs that the global travel appetite has not diminished entirely. Cruise lines have no problems selling staterooms for 2021, and reports of some very crowded areas of cities also prove that the wanderlust hasn't disappeared for everyone, even now.

Research

Now more than ever, before you start making vacation plans, you need to do your research. In 2020, you can't expect to travel without problems. You might be able to easily travel into a country, for example, but find that it's not so easy to travel back. Be aware that you might face mandatory quarantine rules and that negative COVID-19 test results might be the only way out of an enforced stay at home.

The rules can change quickly as the situation evolves. It's important to be aware of the rules and laws both in your destination country as well as when you come back. The United Kingdom, for example, has imposed and lifted travel restrictions on many European countries throughout the pandemic.

I would recommend only making exact plans just before departure. The best way of doing this is to limit the period between planning your vacation and actually going on your vacation. With the rules constantly changing as the virus continues to spread throughout the world, it makes little sense to plan for a vacation too far in the future that might not happen if things change.

Alternatively, you can make flexible bookings to make sure your plans can change on the go if needed. Book hotel rooms that can be cancelled close to your check-in date. The larger hotel chains in particular are now very lenient when it comes to cancellations and many will even reimburse pre-paid non-refundable rooms if you have a genuine reason for not turning up. Sites like Airbnb are less relaxed, with COVID-19 listed as unacceptable excuse for cancelling your trip. While hotel chains are more flexible now, this will likely change if the crisis continues to hold the travel industry in its grip. Research the terms and conditions carefully when booking to avoid having to pay for hotel rooms you end up not being able to use.

The European Union has launched a special website that lists all travel restrictions and applicable rules for its member countries. On the website, you can select any EU member state and see all of the rules and exceptions specific to it. The website also shows whether you have to wear a face mask, are required to social distance, and any other rule that might apply, for example, in bars and restaurants.

Some destinations even go so far as to demand that tourists visiting them have already had the coronavirus and therefore have some degree of immunity. In August, CNN reported that the Fernando de Noronha archipelago off the coast of Brazil had reopened for tourists that are able to "present the result of a positive PCR test (showing presence of the virus) that is at least 20 days old, or the result of the serological test showing the presence of antibodies against Covid"[50].

INSIDER TIP: The EU has launched a very useful website that lists up-to-date information on rules and restriction in all member states: https://reopen.europa.eu/.

Borders

During the dark days of the coronavirus crisis, many countries completely shut their borders to prevent the virus from spreading. In Europe, strict lockdowns were imposed and the spread of the virus was successfully slowed down. By mid-May, many travel restrictions had been lifted and most hotels, restaurants, and bars were able to welcome guests again in early June. However, the situation deteriorated again. There were new outbreaks throughout the continent and restrictions were put back in place. Although borders are not formally shut while I started writing this, restrictions applied based on where you live. As of mid-August, residents of Spain are no longer able to freely travel through the EU. Other countries were added to travel bans that are mostly unilateral decisions and by mid-September, it was once again impossible to move freely within Europe.

In July, I flew to Copenhagen, Denmark, for a short business trip as I had done many times before the crisis. After landing, we couldn't leave the airplane through the regular jet bridge exit and had to exit the plane through the back, where we hopped straight onto a bus. That bus brought us to a dedicated part of the airport where border control had been reintroduced for travelers coming from Schengen countries, an area in which border controls were abolished in 1999.

At the makeshift border control, a long line formed. The line was long because my fellow passengers and I had to practice social distancing as we waited for the Danish border force to allow us in. That this was a very serious situation became clear when two girls in the line found out that they couldn't enter Denmark as they had traveled from a country that was labeled a "risk country". Despite screaming and swearing at the officials, they were forced to wait for the first plane back.

With lots of countries taking their own decisions, rather than coordinated responses, international travel and border restrictions as a result of the pandemic are more complicated than any of us can remember. Border control posts at both airports and on the highways can be time consuming and are very strict. Rapidly changing rules make it hard to know for sure that you are abiding with all the applicable rules even if you checked them before you left.

All summer we have seen reports about traffic jams at borders between EU member states. These borders, usually completely open with no checks at all, have now become a serious hurdle for vacationers. The situation got really bad when Austria imposed new and stricter rules on tourists returning from Croatia on August 22. All returning vacationers needed to register with authorities at the border. This resulted in traffic jams of up to twelve hours, according to Austrian media[51].

You are often not allowed to travel when there's a large number of cases in the country that issued your passport. Denmark closed the border for "travelers in regions where the infection rate is above 50 new infections per 100,000 inhabitants per week"[52]. Other countries have similar rules in place and some are even stricter. The United Kingdom puts countries on their so-called quarantine list when "a country's rate of infection exceeds 20 cases per 100,000 people over seven days", the BBC reports[53].

Flying

COVID-19 has changed how we fly. Sitting in close proximity to each other in a small enclosed area is not as attractive anymore. Initial research has shown that the virus does not spread easily in the air, although these claims are disputed by others. The initial research deems risk of infections on an airplane as relatively small due to the way the air flows and is filtered, as well as precautionary measures taken like the mandatory use of face masks.

Since the lockdowns eased, I've boarded three different planes with two different airlines. On one hand, airports are quieter and the security and check-in process is smoother than before. On the other, airplanes are full and the boarding process is confusing. There's also no in-flight service; you might get a bottle of water if you're lucky.

Measures at the airport

Just like flying before the pandemic, your journey starts at the airport. You still have to check in, go through security, and go through the boarding process. But unlike before the crisis, it's generally much quieter. There are no lines, many shops are closed, and some airports have closed their lounges. From the moment you walk through the doors of an airport, you have to wear a face mask and are asked to clean your hands by using the hand gel dispensers that are available throughout the terminal.

Airports and airlines are doing their utmost to minimize personal contact. Checking in for your flight might happen fully online, which means that it's possible that you're no longer able to check in at the airport. While budget airlines such as Ryanair have always charged extra for those using airport check-in, online check-ins are now becoming the norm for everyone.

Physical contact will be limited everywhere. The only personal belongings that airport staff will touch are the essentials, such as your passport, boarding pass, and your luggage to attach the tags. Almost all the members of staff you encounter, for example at the baggage drop off or at security, will be wearing personal protective equipment (PPE) such as plastic gloves and face masks.

As a traveler, you will be expected to be in good health. Temperature checks and general health questionnaires might be mandatory before you board your flight or enter the terminal. Good hygiene, such as frequently washing your hands, will be expected from everyone, with disinfection gel or spray available almost everywhere. There is no excuse to have dirty hands.

Face masks are mandatory at all airports and during your entire flight. You need to wear a face mask as you enter the terminal, go through the check-in process, spend time in the terminal before your flight, and when you board.

For those who are frequent travelers or traveling in business or first class, there is disappointing news. Although you probably want to use your hard-earned privileges like priority check-in, priority boarding, and lounge access to help maintain your distance from other passengers, lounges are closed at most airports and those that are still open have adapted their services in line with government regulations. This means that beverages are usually available, but the choice is limited. The warm food buffet has been replaced by a counter where hot dishes are handed out to individuals directly and there's usually no choice in food anymore. Each lounge is different, but my stay at the Lufthansa Senator lounge at Frankfurt Airport was still smooth and comfortable.

Unfortunately, priority boarding is completely unavailable on some airlines. At least on intracontinental flights. Most airlines have introduced other measures to avoid personal contact as much as possible, including boarding passengers with a window seat first, followed by passengers with a middle seat, and those with an aisle seat are asked to board last.

During your flight

It's not just the situation at the airport that has changed, of course. Flights are operated differently as well. While some airlines have made statements about keeping the middle seat empty to maintain space between passengers, this is often not the case, and it's definitely not economically sustainable for the airlines. On all three flights I took in July 2020 with two different airlines, every seat could be booked. I was lucky that I had nobody next to me on two out of three of the flights, but the majority of passengers were not so lucky. Although most flights are not filled to their full capacity, it is best to mentally prepare for full airplanes. It is likely that the majority of passengers will have somebody sitting directly next to them.

Face masks are currently mandatory on most flights. You are expected to wear a face mask during the boarding process as well as for the entire duration of your flight. When and how to wear your face mask differs from airline to airline, and may well change as more research is conducted on the virus and how it spreads.

The only time you will be allowed to take your face mask off during your flight is when you eat or drink. Although there are no specific requirements as to what type of face mask or cover should be used, your nose and mouth need to be covered. Some airlines, such as Scandinavia Airlines, have published some more detailed, slightly conflicting, guidelines[54]:

- We do not require your face mask to be medically approved, neither to have any specific type rating. We consider any regular face mask, that covers both mouth and nose, to be accepted.

- Face masks that are sewn by yourself, or any other type of face mask made from garments, are not accepted.

While at the beginning of the crisis, any and all face coverings were allowed, face masks that have a valve are no longer permitted by many airlines. Valves are not considered safe enough as potentially contaminated air can escape through them. Make sure to check the requirements of your chosen airline before you book.

While you are wearing a face mask, the flight attendants will be wearing them as well. Some airlines have completely wrapped their staff in full PPE, including plastic gowns, face masks and gloves. Flight attendants now look like they are going into a hospital operating room. With different regulations in place at different locations, not all airline crews look the same, but most will at least have face masks and gloves. That was certainly what I personally experienced while flying within Europe.

INSIDER TIP: A face mask can be warm and uncomfortable as it heats up in the airplane. Use a face mask that is not too thick and therefore more comfortable, while also ensuring that it meets the requirements of your airline and helps prevent the virus from spreading.

While the mandatory face masks are the biggest change while flying, the onboard service has become nothing short of a disappointment. There is still service on long-haul flights, but airlines have now halted most food and beverage services on shorter flights. Multiple airlines have argued that the protective measures in place to combat the virus mean it is no longer possible to serve food and beverages to customers. You can prepare for the lack of service by bringing some of your own snacks.

All of this means that traveling business class, even on shorter flights, has become attractive again. Not only will you get food that you no longer get in economy, you also minimize the risk of catching COVID-19 because in business class it's more likely that the middle seat will be kept empty— on Lufthansa at least, this was a decision made by the airline. This means that social distancing is much easier if you are willing to pay extra. My experience is that business class is also emptier than usual due to the downturn in business travel during the pandemic, which makes the luxury class even more attractive.

INSIDER TIP: Without onboard services you might get hungry or thirsty on your flight. We recommend buying snacks and drinks at the airport before boarding.

Despite reports of COVID-19 cases among Transavia staff in Europe[55], it appears that the virus has a hard time spreading on an airplane. In mid-August, media from around the world reported that studies[56] have shown that "the odds of catching COVID-19 on a plane are slimmer than you might think"[57]. Airplanes have a particularly low risk of transmission because the air is refreshed continuously. The risk of transmission is also reduced by HEPA air filters that trap 99.97% of small particles. As we are finalizing this book, some researchers are starting to dispute these findings, arguing that flying during the COVID-19 pandemic might not be as safe as we thought. This might mean that the following information might not hold true to its full extend as we find out more about the virus.

In its coverage on the safety of flights during the pandemic, the BBC cited a study from 2018 by the Emory University in Atlanta: "A droplet-mediated respiratory infectious disease is unlikely to be directly transmitted beyond 1 m from the infectious passenger. Thus, transmission is limited to one row in front of or in back of an infectious passenger," the researchers concluded. One explanation for the limited distance droplets can travel is the air flow within an airplane. According to experts interviewed by the BBC, "the reason droplets cannot travel too far in an airplane is because air flows vertically. It is blown from above your head and evacuated from beneath your feet. That makes the level of propagation of anything in the air quite limited. So a passenger from row one, for example, cannot contaminate someone in row 20."

During your flight, the risk of contamination is limited to those passengers that sit in close proximity to you. Not too surprisingly, research by the renowned US university MIT has shown that by keeping the middle seat empty, the risk of getting infected with COVID-19 on a flight drops significantly. Unfortunately, the world association for airlines, the International Air Transport Association (IATA), has explained that this is economically unfeasible for airlines.

Other researchers say that the safest seat in an airplane during the pandemic is a window seat. Airplanes take fresh outside air in and distribute it from vents on the sides of the cabin. Air flows from the side of the plane to the middle. Since droplets follow these airstreams, it's best to sit as close as possible to the source of the air and that is near the windows. Another advantage of the window seat is that you are further away from people walking down the aisle, limiting your contact with fellow passengers even further[58].

INSIDER TIP: Clean your seat, seatbelt, and table as soon as you board your flight. This reduces the risk of getting infected with the virus by touching infected surfaces. Disinfectant wipes are often distributed by the crew as you board the plane.

Hotels

The day that the lockdown measures in Austria were relaxed, coincided with my birthday. On the very first night that it was possible to stay in a hotel again, my wife and I went on a three-day long weekend trip to Vienna to see close friends. One of the "benefits" of the crisis was that luxury hotels heavily discounted their room rates. The Ritz-Carlton Vienna was very reasonably priced and remained open for business travelers during the entire COVID-19 crisis, since the Austrian government continued to allow those with an urgent business-related reason to travel. Our thinking was that a hotel that had remained open during the crisis must have extensive experience with COVID-19 preventive measures and that thinking was proved correct. While the Ritz-Carlton closely followed the rules, they maintained their excellent service, which was not something we experienced in many other hotels.

Although things have not changed as much as on airplanes and in airports, the experience of staying at a hotel will be different as well. Hotels, like restaurants and bars, have had to adapt to the new reality to ensure the safety of the guests, limiting the spread of the virus by enforcing social distancing, preventing the spread through buffets, and cleaning more thoroughly than before. As a result, some facilities might be closed, lounge chairs are now 6 feet (2 m) apart, and the hotel bar is not what it used to be. Staying at around eight hotels in five different countries, we've seen a wide variety of measures in place.

We encountered the strictest measures at the beautiful Renaissance Tuscany Il Ciocco Resort and Spa. Measures there included body temperature checks, mandatory face masks, and strict hand hygiene as well as social distancing. Information and instructions could be found everywhere on the resort's premises. The most striking example was that the hotel door only opened to healthy visitors. In an extensive welcome letter, the hotel informed their guests that they could only enter the hotel when a device at the front door successfully measured and approved their body temperature. The automated body temperature scanner was actually linked to the entrance door. If your temperature was over 37.5 degrees Celsius, the door wouldn't open, hotel staff would be informed, and you would be taken to a separate area within the hotel while the staff arranged medical support and further testing.

Hotel check-in

As you walk into your hotel, you're likely going to be asked to clean your hands with disinfectant. In some countries, like Germany, you are forced to wear a mandatory face mask during check-in. In Italy, we had to wear a face mask as we walked through the hotel. That meant when exiting your room to go to the pool, restaurant, or bar. You could take your face mask off once you were seated at your table, but had to put it back on as soon as you stood up, even for just going to the toilet.

The rules around face masks change constantly as hotels around the world adjust to the local, regional, and national industry regulations in place . In the United States, face masks are not mandatory nationwide, but Marriott Hotels have made it mandatory to wear face masks in their hotels throughout the United States[59]. Those rules will no doubt change as the pandemic evolves and our knowledge of the coronavirus improves.

Whether you are asked to wear a face mask or not, hotel staff will probably welcome you from behind a see-through plastic wall similar to a money exchange. While the plastic wall at a money exchange company serves to protect the employee from potential robbers, this plastic wall serves as a barrier for the coronavirus.

Hotel facilities

For many tourists, hotels can be a destination in themselves. Large swimming pools, spas, private beaches, lounges, and other facilities are all reasons we're willing to pay extra for some hotels. But due to the ongoing situation, many hotels have been forced to close some of these facilities. What remains open differs per hotel and country. During our stay at the Ritz-Carlton in Vienna, the pool, spa, hotel bar, and one of the restaurants were closed.

While this may be an inconvenience to some guests, hotels have no other choice but to close some of their facilities to minimize the risk of exposure to the virus. Hotels also have to close some facilities to reduce their expenditure at a time when they are operating with fewer guests than normal. A hotel that has five bars but only a third of its usual guests will likely have to close one or more bars for economic reasons.

Some hotels offer lounge access, so that frequent travelers and guests staying in premium rooms can enjoy free beverages as well as free snacks. Most of these lounges have closed during the pandemic, but the premium rooms are still sold. We even encountered rooms with "lounge access" in the description despite the fact that most lounges remained shut throughout the summer of 2020. None of the lounges in the hotels that we visited were open. Some offered vouchers for free drinks instead, while others opted for a makeshift kiosk at reception.

Most of us also use hotel reviews to help decide which hotels are good and which ones aren't so great. But these reviews are mostly based on traveler experiences from before the pandemic. A great review about a beautiful swimming pool is fantastic, if you're actually able to enjoy it. That swimming pool might be closed, minibars might be empty, and the spa might only offer one treatment instead of 50.

The combination of health and safety with the economic viability of hotel facilities with reduced guest numbers could cause disappointments. Most hotels are doing their best to communicate what will be open and closed when you arrive at the hotel. Staff will be eager to make your stay as enjoyable as possible, despite any closures. Unfortunately, not all of the information is available on hotel websites or booking sites before you arrive. We highly recommend verifying that the facilities you intend to use are open by calling the hotel before you book.

INSIDER TIP: Hotel websites and booking websites are not always reliable during the pandemic. Call your hotel before you book to find out which facilities are open and closed.

Hotel breakfast

One aspect of traveling during a pandemic that is likely to disappoint any experienced traveler is hotel breakfast. COVID-19 has brought an end to buffet-style dining in lots of places and hotel breakfasts are no exception. This is not without good reason. A Japanese experiment showed just how quickly the coronavirus can spread through a buffet-style restaurant. In the experiment, a buffet was set up and ten participants were asked to serve themselves from it. An invisible fluorescent paint, representing the virus, was sprayed onto the hands of one participant. After enjoying the buffet for 30 minutes, researchers turned off the light to see how the virus had spread through the buffet and who was "infected". The results were shocking: the virus had been transferred through the buffet onto other people's hands and it was even found on the faces of three participants.

With the risk of infection clear, hotels have been forced to find alternatives that allow them to continue to serve quality food, or even proper dining experiences, without the same risks. Most hotel kitchens and restaurants have been designed to operate a buffet, so that challenge is not an easy one to overcome. On our travels since May, we experienced three different solutions:

1. Switching to "à la carte"

2. Plastic-wrapped or served buffet

3. Takeout breakfast

Switching to "à la carte"

The best breakfast experience we had during the pandemic was at the Ritz-Carlton in Vienna. Breakfast was served in one of the hotel's restaurants: DSTRIKT Steakhouse. The hotel offered an extensive à la carte breakfast menu that had something for everyone: from pancakes to sausages and from fruit to cheese. If there was anything you really craved that wasn't on the menu, the experienced kitchen staff would make it happen anyhow. The menu was so good and the service so smooth that we wondered whether there had even been a buffet before COVID-19. The Ritz-Carlton absolutely nailed it. If the buffet never returns to this hotel, it would be just great.

We also received à la carte breakfast at Hotel Lido Blu in Lago di Garda Italy, where we had to fill out a form similar to the room service breakfast menu. At the independent, four-star hotel situated directly at the lake, the staff seemed to be a little overwhelmed by the relatively large number of guests. There were two restaurant staff members that had to provide services to a full terrace. Although they worked hard, they couldn't keep up, which meant you had to wait for your morning coffee and desired breakfast items for quite a long time. Enjoying the magnificent view for a little longer than expected isn't necessarily a problem when on vacation, but waiting is not a luxury most business travelers can afford. The menu itself was extensive and the quality was OK, but it's clear from this experience that à la carte service requires more kitchen and serving staff to facilitate it than the standard buffet.

Overall this is a fantastic alternative to buffet breakfast, but not every hotel can pull it off. In some cases, it can even be a major improvement if the hotel is capable of offering services like the Vienna Ritz-Carlton, but for many other hotels it will be very difficult without increased staff and costs. It's relatively easy for a kitchen to provide quality food to a few guests but à la carte is not easily scalable. Once tourism starts to pick up more quickly, these hotels may begin to struggle..

Plastic-wrapped or served buffet

On two occasions on our travels, hotels continued to offer a buffet-style breakfast. These buffets were adjusted to help prevent the spread of the coronavirus but were still buffets nonetheless. We have dubbed them "COVID-19 buffet breakfasts". The first time we encountered a COVID-19 buffet breakfast was at the Sheraton Carlton Nürnberg. It has, so far, been the worst breakfast experience we've had since the pandemic began. The choices were very limited, and every single slice of ham, bread or fruit was encased in Saran Wrap. With Germany banning single-use plastics as of 2021[60] and others looking to discourage their use, this can't be a long-term solution anywhere. Not only were our options limited, it seemed that the hotel had tried to offset the higher costs of plastic wrapping each item by choosing cheaper, lower quality food. Either that or the breakfast was never any good and they just wrapped their regular, low quality food in plastic. This was our first visit, so we can't know for sure.

The COVID-19 buffet breakfast experience was completely different at the Renaissance hotel in Tuscany. Although smaller than a normal buffet, there was plenty of choice and the hotel didn't opt for cheap, low quality food. The main difference at this buffet is that you cannot take your own items. Instead, restaurant staff wearing face masks operated the buffet on your behalf. The food was on display and was served to you in the portion size you desired, but aside from some single-portion milk bottles and yogurts, you couldn't touch anything yourself before it was on your plate. This hybrid solution between eating à la carte and cruising the good old buffet seemed to work fairly well. A few extra dishes, made to order, would make this setup the perfect compromise.

Takeout

Another form of breakfast we encountered was one that you take away. At Element Frankfurt, hotel guests can no longer go to the restaurant for the traditional buffet. Instead, the restaurant provides a paper bag with a sandwich to your liking, a juice box, and an apple. While this isn't the breakfast experience many would like to enjoy on vacation, it is at least safe and even beats the Sheraton plastic-wrapped buffet in our opinion. The takeout bag at this particular hotel wasn't that great—it had a rotten apple—but the concept of a breakfast to go, perhaps with a pre-order system, is definitely one that works in the new normal.

The return of the buffets

Despite all of these new ways of serving breakfast, the economically best option for hotels will always be the buffet. The buffet allows hotels to provide lots of options for its guests while minimizing the number of staff needed to run it. This helps explain why even just a few months after the first peak of the pandemic, we started to see the return of the regular buffet breakfast. At the Marriott Copenhagen, a standard buffet breakfast is available again to guests. To touch the buffet, you need to sanitize your hands and wear plastic gloves, so none of the guests directly touch the food and the choice of products is back to pre-COVID-19 standards. It was one of the best solutions we've come across so far.

We came across another Marriott buffet in Heidelberg. Guests were asked to pick a time slot to avoid too many people eating breakfast at the same time. Upon arrival at the restaurant, guests were also asked to fill out a form that would enable smooth contact-tracing in case one of the guests at the restaurant later tested positive for the virus. Except for multiple hand-sanitizer stations, the hotel had returned to a regular buffet breakfast including eggs, meats, cereals, and salmon.

Conclusion

Some hotels have struggled with breakfast as COVID-19 forces them to abandon old concepts. On our travels, we have experienced both perfect and disappointing solutions. The pandemic offers hotels an opportunity to exceed their guest's expectations and allows them to explore new ideas. After all, regardless of whether you're on vacation or on a business trip, you want to start the day as positively and strongly as possible. While we might have been critical toward some approaches, we know that everyone is trying to find the best possible way of servicing their guests during these challenging times. We were always welcomed by friendly and accommodating staff that was trying to do their best for us. In any case, the regular buffet is likely to make a quick comeback as soon as the situation allows for it, as we have already seen in places like Heidelberg.

INSIDER TIP: Hotel breakfast is not what it was before. Don't trust the information in online reviews as they are likely from before the pandemic. It is best to contact the hotel directly and ask what their breakfast looks like before booking.

Other types of transport

Even if you travel by train, bus, or car rather than flying, you will notice differences from before the pandemic. When you travel by train, you're now required to wear a face mask in most parts of the world. And the same goes for buses and taxis. In taxis, both the driver and passengers are required to wear a face mask. Additionally, some countries limit the number of passengers from different households that can ride in a taxi together. There might also be social distancing rules in place when you travel in public transport, including leaving certain seats empty. Thankfully, most trains and buses are emptier than before the pandemic, making this much easier to do.

While traveling by car, the biggest challenge in Europe are the borders. Openborders are one of the main achievements and advantages of the European Union, but the crisis has put them back in place. With continuously changing rules, border controls can take a long time, resulting in massive traffic jams.

On August 22, the Austrian government changed the rules for visitors returning from Croatia[61]. Unlike in the days and weeks before, returning tourists suddenly needed to be registered as they re-entered their home country. This meant thousands of unprepared tourists being asked to provide personal information at the border, a very slow process. The consequences for traffic was disastrous. Traffic jams of over 12 hours formed at the border and the situation only improved when those who were merely passing through Austria, rather than ending their journey there, were waved through without registration. The traffic jam was cut from 12 hours to "just" six hours.

Although this example from Austria is not very common, it shows us two things. Firstly, that borders and border control made acome back throughout Europe, and being checked at the border is not something Europeans are used to when they travel between EU member states. Secondly it shows us just how quickly the situation can change. According to media covering the border situation, most of the returning tourists in the 12-hour traffic jams weren't even aware of the new rules.

The situation on the roads has become difficult to predict. More people now seem to travel by car than in airplanes. In the United States, the AAA was unable to do a forecast for the Memorial Day weekend for the first time in 20 years[62]. Meanwhile, in Europe, serious traffic jams formed on what is normally referred to as "Black Saturday" in France and Germany[63]. On Saturday August 1, French authorities reported about 760 kilometers (472 miles) of traffic jams on French roads, though this was only 2 kilometers (1.23 miles) less than what was reported the year before, without COVID-19. A week later, the situation was even worse as 820 kilometers (510 miles) of traffic jams were reported compared to 720 kilometers (447 miles) the year before.

Tourist attractions

Traveling in 2020 has its challenges. COVID-19 has changed everything. From corona tests upon arrival in Greece[64] to mandatory face masks in most southern European countries, it will feel nothing like your last vacation. We have already written about the challenges we had with booking hotel rooms[65] and finding a good hotel breakfast. But what about what tourists like to do most? What is it like to visit tourist attractions?

The best news is that most tourist attractions in Europe have now reopened, but that news comes with some caveats. None of them are open like they used to be, since they too have to do what they can to help prevent the spread of the virus. Tourist attractions are doing their best to limit contact between visitors as well as staff. This starts with buying tickets. Ticket offices and even ticket machines are often closed, and you have to go online to get in. Over the summer, we visited two world famous tourist attractions: the famous Schönbrunn Palace in Vienna, and the Leaning Tower of Pisa. We bought both tickets online, which turned out to be an essential decision, as ticket kiosks were all closed and the many ticket machines at the palace were not operating.

Most attractions have reduced the number of tickets available to tourists and aren't operating at full capacity yet, since that would mean that tourists aren't able to distance from each other. In most cases, tickets need to be purchased well in advance as well as online. You can no longer show up at an attraction and expect to get in. At Schönbrunn Palace and at the Leaning Tower of Pisa, the purchased tickets were timed entry tickets, only valid at a certain given time on a specific day.

At the Leaning Tower of Pisa, our time slot was 12:15. Every 15 minutes, the tower staff allowed a group of about 20 tourists to ascend the stairs. As per the conditions set out on our ticket, we arrived about 15 minutes before our time slot and had to stand in a short line at the bottom of the tower because the staff was slightly behind schedule. A family who arrived shortly after didn't appear to have gotten the memo about buying advance timed entry tickets. While the mother of the family stayed in line to keep their favorable place, the rest of the family went to the kiosk to buy tickets and soon returned with a sad look on their faces. There were no tickets available anymore. All the timeslots were fully booked. Their plan to get into the tower was thwart by bad planning.

That family taught us the importance of doing your homework. In 2020, you can't expect to show up without a ticket and be allowed into any tourist attraction. Pre-booking tickets requires some research and planning before you leave for your vacation, but it's worth it. When you do manage to get into your chosen attraction, you'll probably find that some things are a little different inside too.

Hand hygiene and temperature checks

At both Schönbrunn Palace and the Leaning Tower of Pisa, there was an abundance of measures put in place to prevent the spread of the virus. Keeping your hands clean is easy when there are hand-sanitizer stations everywhere. At the palace in Vienna, there were even hand sanitizers that you could operate with your feet without the need to touch the dispenser itself. We were also frequently reminded to wash our hands. While we didn't encounter temperature checks ourselves, we have seen multiple reports of tourist attractions where a quick temperature check was done before allowing tourists inside and we saw this practice in place at several large chain shops like the Apple store in Vienna and the Hard Rock Café in Florence as well.

Social distancing

Social distancing is enforced in different ways in different places, and what measures are in place depends on the attraction. At both the tower and the palace, enforced walking paths—meaning that you can only walk one direction and can't return to a part of the building you've already seen—were in place even before the coronavirus stopped mass tourism, but we see these being introduced in more attractions as they are reopening. The idea behind mandatory walking directions is that it makes it easier for visitors to keep their distance from each other. When people move back and forth in relatively small spaces, they will block pathways and create jams. Mandatory directions make the flow of crowds easier. With that in mind, I expect that some of these measures will stay well beyond COVID-19.

At the Leaning Tower of Pisa, there was another measure put in place to help people keep their distance. Every visiting group received a COVID-19 gadget: a lanyard with a light attached to it. When there was enough distance between you and the next group, the light would be green, but as soon as one of the other gadgets got too close to yours, it would turn red and start vibrating to alert you. This was a really smart way to make you aware of your distance from others while also helping you steer clear of other visitors on the tower's narrow staircases where it's difficult to see people coming. One downside of these devices was that when parents gave the gadget to their kids, it became a toy. Kids on our tour played a dangerous game: deliberately making the gadget turn red by getting close to other groups.

Face masks

Face masks might also be mandatory, depending on the attraction. When we visited Schönbrunn Palace, we had to wear our face masks the entire Grand Tour of the emperor's palace, though the situation changed as Austria's case numbers fell, but the numbers have since risen again and face masks may be reintroduced. The rules change constantly and you should always be prepared to wear face masks by carrying one with you at all times.

In Italy, the situation was different. The country was one of the hardest hit nations in Europe, and strict measures were in place during our visit that are likely to stay in place for some time. One of those measures is that face masks are absolutely mandatory. Wearing a face mask might not be comfortable during the ascent of 294 steps in the scorching Italian sun, but it does help protect staff and other visitors.

Cashless payments

The exchange of coins and bills is an easy way for the virus to spread between visitors and staff and many tourist attractions have put measures in place to prevent that. One of those measures is to stop accepting cash payments, asking you to pay with a card or even contactless payment, with a near-field communication (NFC) enabled card or through your phone.

Closed facilities

It's not just the ticket kiosks that are closed. Souvenir shops, information desks, and sometimes even the restrooms may be closed as well. Each attraction, country, and region has their own set of rules. Attractions will close down certain facilities to avoid the virus spreading, but also because there are fewer guests to makes the running of additional facilities worthwhile financially. At Schönbrunn Palace, shops at the entrance and exit were unmanned and closed. While we didn't encounter closed restrooms ourselves, it's something to keep in mind and prepare for where possible.

Low visitor numbers

The biggest change at tourist attractions is the absence of mass tourism. No matter where you decide to go, it's likely to be far quieter than before the pandemic. Traveling in 2020 feels more like the experience tourists had 30 years ago, before mass tourism conquered the world. But even with fewer fellow tourists, it doesn't mean you don't have to prepare at all. Tickets still sell out quickly as tourist attractions have no choice but to limit their capacity. It also helps to check terms and conditions at the last minute, since rules change quickly. The virus now controls what is open and under what conditions. And always bring a face mask.

Health and safety

At any point in your journey, you could be exposing yourself to COVID-19. Not only can you get sick yourself, but you might take the virus with you or bring it back when your return from your vacation. Some people believe this means that we shouldn't travel at all, but traveling should not be more dangerous than going about your daily business if you take precautions to limit the risks as much as possible.

Health and safety should be your number one concern when traveling during or immediately after the pandemic. You should be aware of the health and safety of those you come into contact with in your destination country and your home country in addition to your own health and safety.

That means you need to make yourself familiar with the rules and regulations applicable for your destination by doing some research before you go. In addition, there are some general guidelines that will make your vacation as safe as possible.

Face masks

Face masks are mandatory in some countries, while in others there are almost no rules. When we were in Italy, face masks were mandatory almost everywhere—in supermarkets, bars, and restaurants as well as any tourist attraction you visit. In other countries, face masks are either still not mandatory or were introduced very late. I would recommend always wearing a face mask in any of these situations. When you travel, you are a visitor: wear a face mask to protect others as well as reducing the risk of infection for yourself.

Social distancing

Stay safe by staying away from people. COVID-19 spreads easily when we are close to or make physical contact with each other. Don't shake hands, don't hug, and don't kiss people outside your household. It's difficult when you visit friends and family, but it's a small sacrifice worth making if we want to return to normal as soon as possible.

Keeping away from others is not always easy when you're in a crowded area. I would therefore recommend completely avoiding busy areas. When it's not possible to stay away from others at a tourist attraction, for example on a bridge or at a viewing point, find something else to do instead and return when the crowds have gone. Don't visit landmarks or museums when you know they are likely to be busy. Mornings are always better than afternoons.

While it's perfectly fine to have a drink and enjoy dinner in a restaurant, it's not OK to do so when it means getting too close to others. Bars and clubs might be open, but it is your responsibility to ensure your own safety and that of others around you. Remember, when people have a few drinks and lose their inhibitions, social distancing gets even harder.

Act responsibly

As a tourist who may unknowingly bring the virus with them, you pose a risk to the city or country you visit. To minimize the impact you have on your destination, you should at the very least follow all local rules. COVID-19 rules differ percountry and can even be different between regions, but it's vitally important that you understand and follow them. Not only can you be fined or arrested if you do not comply, it also is the right thing to do to keep everyone (including yourself) safe.

Ensure that you know what the local rules are. In general, ensure that you know where and when face masks are mandatory and what social distancing rules you need to adhere to. Always make sure you carry a face mask with you.

GLOBAL TRAVEL CALENDAR

January

January is one of the slowest travel months around the entire world. After the end of the holiday season, which for some extends into the first week of the year, global tourism comes to a standstill. January brings some of the lowest airfares and hotel prices of the year, but weather in the Northern Hemisphere is not great. The opposite is, of course, the case in the Southern Hemisphere, where temperatures are good and traveling is still popular and common.

Europe: Cold and wet weather, with slow crowds. Hotel prices and airfares are extremely low. City trips are not popular, because of low temperatures and short days. Ski resorts and Spanish and Portuguese islands in the Atlantic Ocean can get busy.

USA: The cold winter weather makes tourism slow down in the United States, but sunnier destinations like Hawaii and Florida are still relatively busy. This is a cheap time of year for city trips in the states, so it's an excellent time to visit big cities which are normally busy and expensive, such as New York and Los Angeles.

Australia: Summer holidays bring peak season to the Southern Hemisphere. January is an extremely busy month in Australia, throughout the entire nation. It's busy, but the weather is fantastic.

South America: This period is the height of summer in South America, but it's also the rainy season in many of the continent's nations. If you want to visit South America during this month, Chile is a good bet.

Asia: Asian January weather is impossible to summarise, but many of the countries have a hot, sunny climate during the month. It's a great time to visit countries such as Thailand and Malaysia, but countries like Japan and Korea can be cold.

Recommended destinations: Canary Islands, Los Angeles, Chile or Thailand

February

February remains a slow travel month across the globe. Apart from during the Valentine's Day weekend, most destinations see few tourists. That said, winter weather combined with school vacations in Europe do attract lots of tourists to the Alps and other winter sports areas.

Europe: Peak season for winter sports. Busy in the Alps and in other mountainous regions, while the rest of the continent remains in hibernation. For warmer cities in the south of Europe, this can be a good time to visit, with low prices, low tourist numbers and relatively warm weather.

USA: Slow travel month, except for some ski resorts or extremely sunny destinations.

Australia: Summer holidays bring peak season to the Southern Hemisphere. February is a very busy month in Australia. Domestic tourism does slow down a little compared with January, while international tourism increases slightly.

South America: Again, this isn't a great time to visit South America. Though the weather is warm, it can often be very rainy too.

Asia: It depends where you are. China and other mountainous regions can be very cold, while warmer parts of places such as Malaysia, India and The Philippines are at their best during this period.

Recommended destinations: Ibiza, Singapore or Sri Lanka

March

While the Southern Hemisphere prepares for winter, the Northern Hemisphere is enjoying the first warmer days of the year. Although global tourism starts to pick up, March remains a slow month in most of the world. Many destinations have a relatively low number of tourists, but the weather can be surprisingly warm in, for example, Europe. March is the last month for winter sports in the Alps and the last warm peak season month in the Caribbean.

Although the Easter weekend sometimes falls in March, there are generally no big school vacations and only a few public holidays. It's a quiet month but you must check the weather and prepare for quickly changing weather. One exception is the United States, as March is Spring Break month for most colleges and universities. Keep that in mind when you decide to travel to popular spring break destinations in Florida!

Europe: The continent is warming up, but March is relatively a slow travel month, with the exception of some warmer southern cities. It's the last month for winter sports.

USA: Except for Spring Break, March is a slow travel month.

Australia: While summer is coming to an end, it is still peak season, as tourists flock to Australia to enjoy the cooler part of the summer period.

South America: This can be a good time to visit South America. As the rains start to slow and the temperatures begin to slightly increase, it can be a good time to visit South America on a budget.

Asia: An excellent time to visit Asia, as crowds largely aren't at their biggest and temperatures throughout the continent are largely pretty good. Japan's cherry blossom season hits in March.

Recommended destinations: Japan, Jamaica, Ecuador and southern Italy

April

Easter is the first big test for destinations suffering from overtourism. With almost all western Europeans (adults and kids alike) having vacation time during this period, Europe can be remarkably busy. The Easter weekend is one of the most popular off-season weekends to travel. Long weekend trips and domestic day-trippers will make destinations across the European continent extremely busy. Expect long lines, traffic jams and soaring hotel prices. Outside of the Easter weekend, April is a relatively slow month. Outside of Europe, the Easter effect is not felt as strongly.

Europe: Extremely busy around the Easter weekend, especially in major cities. Outside of Easter, April is a great shoulder season month to travel.

USA: April is still slow season and a perfect month to visit sunny destinations like Hawaii or Florida. It's also a great time for city breaks.

Australia: It can get busy around Easter, but April is otherwise pretty quiet in the nation. If you're keen for an Australia break, April can be a great time, with good temperatures.

South America: This is one of the best periods to travel in South America. Throughout the whole continent, temperatures are moderate and weather is very tolerable. Crowds begin to pick up after April.

Asia: April is a great time to visit Asia. The rainy season hasn't yet hit the tropical parts of Asia, while the more northern parts of the nation are starting to heat up. Throughout the vast majority of the nation, weather is great, but crowds can be high.

Recommended destinations: Bolivia, China and the Netherlands

May

Although May is far from peak season in the region, travel starts to pick up again across the Northern Hemisphere. Popular destinations can get seriously crowded around the several public holidays in Europe. Cities like Paris, Rome and Berlin get especially busy around European Labour Day, Ascension and Whitsun. While weather in the Northern Hemisphere improves, the Southern Hemisphere gets ready for winter.

Europe: May is a good month to travel in Europe, especially in cities and mountainous regions, but expect big crowds around the public holidays.

USA: The weather improves and tourism starts to pick up slowly. Memorial Day weekend (the last weekend of May) can be very crowded.

Australia: While not so busy in the south, it can get busy in the north around the many public holidays in May.

South America: This is peak season in some parts of South America, as weather is at its best throughout pretty much the entire continent. It will be busy, but the weather is fantastic in cities, beaches and mountains.

Asia: May is great in Asia, especially in the east, where the blooms and blossoms of spring are at their peak. It can be a little rainy in the tropical areas of Asia, as the monsoon season begins in mid-May.

Recommended destinations: England, Central Asia and Peru

June

June is arguably the best month to travel in the Northern Hemisphere. Warm weather and low levels of rain make traveling very comfortable, while the largest crowds have not yet arrived in the region's most popular destinations. That said, there are some public holidays to be aware of in Europe, which – along with school vacations at the end of the month – can make some periods busy.

Europe: June is a relatively warm month and most schools are still in session until the end of the month. As a result, you get good weather conditions and low crowds. June is a great time to be in Europe.

USA: With most schools still in session, peak season hasn't yet arrived in the United States. Warm weather and the absence of hurricane season make it a good month to travel.

Australia: June is low season in most of Australia, so it's a great time to visit if you want to avoid crowds. The temperatures aren't great, but they're certainly tolerable. It's the perfect time to visit the Great Barrier Reef.

South America: weather is great throughout much of the continent, and this is the last month to enjoy travel in most parts of the country. If you want to visit the Andes, June marks the start of the best period to do it.

Asia: while tropical areas in Asia can be pretty wet during June, northern parts of Asia are excellent during this period, with temperatures which are perfect for city sightseeing.

Recommended destinations: Australia's Great Barrier Reef, Greenland and Turkey

July

July is one of the busiest travel months of the year. With children in almost the entire Northern Hemisphere out of school, families have an opportunity to travel – and they use it. In the United States, Independence Day results in a travel peak early in the month, while most European families tend to travel later in the month. Even in the Southern Hemisphere, where it is now the middle of winter, international tourism starts to pick up.

July is when many travel destinations truly begin to suffer from overtourism. The first part of the month is better than the second, but if you can avoid traveling in July or August, I would recommend doing so.

Europe: July brings peak season to the continent. Destinations get extremely busy as the weather is at its best. We recommend avoiding the month completely or opting for destinations which are less popular, such as the Balkans.

USA: The weekend surrounding the Fourth of July marks the beginning of the busy summer travel season. Tourism hits full swing during the second part of the month.

Australia: Although July falls within Australia's winter, Europe's peak travel season does result in heavy tourism in Australia during July and August. The north of the country in particular can see heavy crowds.

South America: It's winter in the Southern Hemisphere, but it's still pretty busy. Travelers from the Northern Hemisphere, especially those with kids off school for the summer, still travel to Central and South America during this period. Destinations around the equator are especially popular.

Asia: For city breaks in northern parts of Asia, this is the best time. It can be a fantastic time to visit some of the bigger cities in places like Japan,

Korea and China, while Central Asia's mountainous regions are brilliant during July.

Recommended destinations: Canada, Mexico, Albania and the Alps

August

Worldwide travel hits its peak in August. The last weeks of July and the first weeks of August are by far the busiest travel weeks in Europe - roads and highways are jammed as tourists travel throughout the continent. Airports also get extremely busy. It's equally busy in the United States.

Destinations like Paris and Dubrovnik become extremely crowded. Cruise ships also roam European waters, bringing in even more tourists to the already busy destinations. Venice's official travel website recommends that tourists pick other periods to travel.

Europe: Warm summer weather results in massive crowds across the continent. If you can avoid this month, I would recommend staying at home and traveling at a different time. Even Europe's less popular destinations can be very busy during this period.

USA: Early August is peak season in the United States. Cities, resorts and most other popular destinations are very busy. If you like to avoid crowds, it's not a great time.

Australia: Although August falls within Australia's winter, Europe's travel season does result in tourism picking up in July and August in the north of Australia. Cities such as Sydney and Melbourne can be very busy, as can the most popular beach areas.

South America: As in July, travelers from the Northern Hemisphere still travel to Central and South America. Destinations around the equator are especially popular.

Asia: if you want to visit mountainous regions in the non-tropical areas of Asia, August is the ideal time. If you're planning on visiting the tropical areas, don't visit during August – you'll be hit by very disruptive monsoons.

Recommended destinations: Iceland, Argentina and Tajikistan

September

As schools reopen their doors in September, many families are no longer free to travel. September therefore marks the end of peak season and the beginning of the increasingly popular shoulder season. In the United States, tourism drops considerably, while many destinations in Europe remain busy in the first weeks and weekends.

Europe: September marks the start of shoulder season. However, large numbers of tourists at the beginning of the month mean it can still be busy.

USA: The summer vacation season is unofficially marked as over by the arrival of Labour Day weekend. As a result, it's less crowded in the states even though the weather is still good. Hurricane season makes Florida and the Caribbean region unattractive for many travelers.

Australia: Like the rest of the world, September marks the start of shoulder season in Australia. It can be a great time to travel if you want to avoid crowds.

South America: September is a great time to visit South America. Temperatures are pleasant throughout the whole continent, crowds are relatively low and spring begins to blossom in some areas.

Asia: This is when monsoon weather begins to draw to a close, making it a great time to visit tropical areas of Asia before the crowds hit.

Recommended destinations: Croatia, China, Brazil and Scotland

October

Global warming is changing the global travel calendar. October always used to be too cold and wet to enjoy a good vacation, but it's now – in many places - a perfect month to travel. You can expect low crowds and relatively good weather, perfect if you like to enjoy good climes without many other tourists.

Europe: Except for some school holidays and a few public holidays, October is a relatively quiet month on the European continent. If you feel like a city break in Europe, now is a good time before it becomes too cold.

USA: October is a quiet travel month, making it a great time to visit cities.

Australia: October brings almost no crowds to Australia, but the weather remains pleasant in most places. If you want to visit Australia without countless crowds and soaring temperatures, October is a great time.

South America: October brings spring to South America, so it can be a great time to visit if you want to explore cities or low-level hiking destinations. It's also a great time to avoid crowds.

Asia: It's a fantastic time to visit places such as Bangkok, Delhi and other vast, hot cities. Weather is pleasant, and crowds aren't yet at their largest.

Recommended destinations: Berlin, Bangkok, Australia and North Africa

November

November is one of the world's slowest travel months. In the Northern Hemisphere, it's cold and wet, while summer has not yet reached the Southern Hemisphere. Christmas markets attract crowds in cities across Europe, while Thanksgiving causes a travel peak in the United States.

Europe: November brings cold weather and relatively few tourists. Though some of Western Europe's bigger cities begin to celebrate the Christmas period, most cities are quiet. November can be a good month to travel to some of Europe's warmer places, such as the Balkans.

USA: Except for the days surrounding Thanksgiving, November is a slow travel month in the United States. You should expect low crowds and adverse weather conditions, particularly in higher regions.

Australia: November brings few tourists to Australia, but the weather is still pretty good.

South America: Winter fully makes way for spring, but you can still expect pretty low crowds. If you want to explore some of South America's hiking opportunities, now is a pretty good time.

Asia: this is a fantastic time to visit the southern parts of Asia, as temperatures are at their most tolerable. But be warned: these places can be very busy.

Recommended destinations: Cambodia, Myanmar and Australia

December

Christmas shopping and Christmas markets attract some crowds to larger western cities such as New York and London. Meanwhile, winter sports destinations experience some of their busiest weeks, while lots of people also travel to see their loved ones. All of these factors result in a major peak in tourism in the weeks around Christmas. This surge in travel can be felt in most airports throughout the world, and airfares can be even higher than some of the busiest summer weeks.

Europe: City trips, skiing and a peak in travel to see family and friends make the end of December very crowded. Large cities in Western Europe are busy every weekend in December.

USA: The holiday season is one of the busiest times of the year, especially in major cities such as New York. The festivities are fun during this period, but the crowds can be disruptive.

Australia: While it can get crowded around the Christmas break, December is overall a pretty quiet period in Australia. If you want to enjoy some winter sun, Australia can be a fantastic choice.

South America: December is a good month to visit South America as it marks the start of summer in the Southern Hemisphere. Expect large crowds around the holidays. If you want to explore some of South America's mountainous areas, now can be a fantastic choice.

Asia: In northern parts of Asia, weather can be cold but pleasant. In tropical areas, weather is at its best but busy destinations can be very crowded.

Recommended destinations: Munich, Lapland, Russia and Florida

ACKNOWLEDGMENTS

It was never my intention to write a book. It just happened. During the lockdown, I started writing a guide that we could publish on Avoid-Crowds.com. Somehow, the words came naturally to me and within no time I had written over 30,000 words. After that, I decided to push on turn that "guide" into a real book. But I couldn't do that alone and I have many people to thank.

First and most of all, my wife Mandy has supported me in writing the book and pushing me forward. Mandy shares my passion for travel and, without her, Avoid-Crowds.com wouldn't exist. Many of the memories and anecdotes in the book are not mine but ours. Thank you.

I also want to thank my parents Henk and Marcelle for letting me travel at a young age and encouraging me to explore the world as I grew up. Thank you for all the trips and memories. I hope many more will follow after the pandemic. Dad, thanks too for proofreading the book and your constructive feedback. Mom, thanks for sharing the photos and memories from back in the sixties.

Furthermore, I need to thank Kate Nascimento for the amazing copy-editing she has done. It isn't easy to take my texts and transform them into something readable. The great book design is by Milos Jevremovic, while the infographics and designs in the book are done by Immaculate Studios. The icons used are from Flaticon.com and designed and used by Immaculate Studios. Immaculate Studios also designed a fantastic alternative cover, which I long considered using. I also hired freelance writer Paul McDougal to help finish the global travel calendar, because there was no inspiration left to do that myself.

Last but not least, a massive thank you to all those that use Avoid-Crowds.com and the bloggers and journalists that write about our website!

CITED SOURCES

1

https://ajuntament.barcelona.cat/turisme/sites/default/files/informe_ciutat_de_barcelona_2018_1.pdf

2 https://data.london.gov.uk/dataset/number-international-visitors-london - accessed in May 2020

3 https://www.tourismalliance.com/downloads/TA_408_435.pdf

4 https://www2.deloitte.com/content/dam/Deloitte/pt/Documents/transportation-infrastructures-services/Portuguese%20Hospitality%20Atlas%202017.pdf

5 https://fortune.com/2019/07/02/july-4th-travel-fourth-of-july-airports/

6 https://www.sn.at/salzburg/wirtschaft/so-viele-skifahrer-wie-noch-nie-weihnachtsferien-bescherten-rekorde-auf-salzburgs-pisten-81508972

7 https://www.forbes.com/sites/jenniferleighparker/2020/05/22/meet-the-startup-aiming-to-solve-overtourism/#4bdc54d15144

8 https://www.travelweekly.com/Travel-News/Hotel-News/Ticket-shock-Theme-park-companies-turning-to-dynamic-ticket-pricing

9 https://www.tripadvisor.co.uk/ShowTopic-g189433-i245-k12839875-Avoiding_the_Crowds-Santorini_Cyclades_South_Aegean.html

10 https://data.worldbank.org/indicator/ST.INT.DPRT?most_recent_value_desc=true

11 https://hbswk.hbs.edu/item/to-buy-happiness-purchase-an-experience#:~:text=Michael%20Norton%20explains%20why%20spending,spending%20it%20on%20new%20products.&text=Conventional%20wisdom%20says%20that%20money%20can't%20buy%20happiness.&text=In%20fact%2C%20research%20shows%20that,spend%20it%20in%20particular%20ways.

[12] https://www.e-unwto.org/doi/pdf/10.18111/9789284420070

[13] https://ourworldindata.org/world-population-growth

[14] https://mk0destinationajcrrq.kinstacdn.com/wp-content/uploads/2020/05/des_report_winter_SoAT_2020_v3-1.pdf

[15] http://www.tourism-master.com/theses/Domestic_and_International_Tourism_in_a_Globalized_World.PDF

[16] http://www.tourism-master.com/theses/Domestic_and_International_Tourism_in_a_Globalized_World.PDF

[17] https://www.mdpi.com/2071-1050/12/5/1729/pdf

[18] https://hbr.org/2019/04/research-when-airbnb-listings-in-a-city-increase-so-do-rent-prices

[19] https://www.bbc.com/news/business-45083954

[20] https://www.parool.nl/nieuws/gemeente-amsterdam-niet-onder-de-indruk-van-belofte-airbnb~baafd930/

[21] https://www.parool.nl/amsterdam/geen-vakantieverhuur-meer-in-deel-centrum~b6f7b3a5/

[22] https://www.eea.europa.eu/media/infographics/co2-emissions-from-passenger-transport/view

[23] https://www.tourismdashboard.org/explore-the-data/cruise-ship/#:~:text=Based%20on%20an%20estimated%20total,dioxide%2Dequivalent%20for%20their%20cruise.

[24] https://ec.europa.eu/environment/emas/takeagreenstep/pdf/BEMP-6-FINAL.pdf

[26] https://www.smithsonianmag.com/science-nature/single-use-plastic-covid-180975312/

[27] https://www.instagram.com/p/B9VHE1WpZ8p/

[28] https://131f4363709c46b89a6ba5bc764b38b9.objectstore.eu/hior/Documenten/Notitie%20Touringcarbeleid%20Amsterdam%202012-2020%20(2012).pdf

[29] https://assets.amsterdam.nl/publish/pages/916171/inspraakversie_touringcar_agenda_oktober_2019.pdf

[30] https://www.e-unwto.org/doi/pdf/10.18111/9789284420070

31 https://avoid-crowds.com/tourists-willing-to-pay-to-avoid-crowds/

32 https://www.bloomberg.com/news/articles/2018-05-01/venice-erects-gates-against-a-flood-of-tourists

33 https://indd.adobe.com/view/a614092f-2162-4a39-97c3-f4d67b0cbe0b

34 https://www.ceicdata.com/en/indicator/italy/visitor-arrivals

35 https://people.com/travel/austrian-village-struggling-to-deal-with-hordes-of-tourists-hallstatt-instagram/ & https://www.theguardian.com/film/shortcuts/2020/jan/06/let-it-go-why-the-mayor-of-hallstatt-is-telling-frozen-fans-to-stay-away

36 https://www.dailymail.co.uk/news/article-7855995/Alpine-village-inspired-Frozen-begs-tourists-stay-away.html

37 https://www.telegraaf.nl/nieuws/455908500/stadswandelingen-in-amsterdam-aan-banden

38 https://edition.cnn.com/travel/article/statue-of-liberty-commercial-tours-new-york/index.html

39 https://www.latimes.com/travel/story/2019-12-27/reconsider-travel-2020-overtourism-crowding

40 https://ourworldindata.org/tourism#:~:text=International%20arrivals%20by%20world%2 0region,-Arrivals%20by%20world&text=The%20United%20Nations%20World%20Tourism,is% 20a%2056%2Dfold%20increase.

41 https://www.at5.nl/artikelen/203344/toeristen-zijn-terug-zo-druk-was-het-vannacht-op-de-wallen

42 https://www.theguardian.com/travel/2020/jul/18/amsterdam-post-lockdown-cycling-a-tourist-free-joy

43 https://www.at5.nl/artikelen/203343/gemeente-roept-op-kom-niet-naar-de-wallen-het-is-te-druk

44 https://nos.nl/artikel/2341041-voorlopig-geen-optredens-van-straatartiesten-in-centrum-amsterdam.html

45 https://www.hartvannederland.nl/nieuws/2020/kalverstraat-eenrichtingsverkeer-drukte/

46 https://twitter.com/DonCeder/status/1284587008858501120

[47] https://www.parool.nl/amsterdam/dit-zijn-de-verscherpte-coronaregels-in-amsterdam~b8c6b805/

[48] https://support.google.com/maps/answer/144339?co=GENIE.Platform%3DDesktop&hl=en

[49] https://www.dailymail.co.uk/travel/travel_news/article-3041513/Save-Florence-mass-tourism-New-campaign-bids-reclaim-city-16million-visitors-monitor-damage-cause.html

[50] https://edition.cnn.com/travel/article/fernando-de-noronha-brazil-reopens-covid-19/index.html

[51] https://orf.at/stories/3178492/

[52] https://um.dk/en/news/newsdisplaypage/?newsid=c730ab75-d4d9-4310-9af8-787af4272f64

[53] https://www.bbc.com/news/explainers-53221896

[54] https://www.flysas.com/en/safe-travel/

[55] https://nltimes.nl/2020/08/24/concerns-covid-infections-among-transavia-staff-report

[56] https://edition.cnn.com/travel/article/odds-catching-covid-19-flight-wellness-scn/index.html & https://www.newscientist.com/article/2252152-how-likely-are-you-to-be-infected-by-the-coronavirus-on-a-flight/

[57] https://www.bbc.com/news/business-52822913#:~:text=They%20filter%20out%2099.97%25%20of,size%20of%20Covid%2D19.%22&text=This%20regular%20flow%20of%20air,path%20of%20any%20airborne%20particles.

[58] https://www.insider.com/window-seat-best-place-to-sit-plane-health-experts-say-2020-6

[59] https://www.hospitalitynet.org/news/4099760.html#:~:text=Marriott%20has%20announced%20that%20all,effect%20on%2027%20July%202020.

[60] https://www.dw.com/en/germany-bans-single-use-plastic-products/a-53932107

[61] https://www.total-croatia-news.com/politics/46015-foreign-ministry-urges-austria-to-find-solution-to-traffic-jams-on-borders & https://www.telegraaf.nl/nieuws/198306613/chaos-aan-sloveens-oostenrijkse-grens-door-nieuwe-coronamaatregel

[62] https://nbc24.com/news/local/for-the-first-time-in-20-years-aaa-will-not-release-travel-forecast

63 https://www.parool.nl/wereld/toch-weer-gewoon-zwarte-zaterdag-met-900-kilometer-file-in-frankrijk~bdaf6e71/

64 https://www.theguardian.com/world/2020/jul/17/greece-offers-british-tourists-a-wary-welcome-back

65 https://avoid-crowds.com/traveling-after-covid-19-choosing-a-hotel/